MW01141879

Agency and Impersonality

Studies in Language Companion Series (SLCS)

The SLCS series has been established as a companion series to *Studies in Language*, International Journal, sponsored by the Foundation "Foundations of Language".

Volume 78

Agency and Impersonality: Their Linguistic and Cultural Manifestations
by Mutsumi Yamamoto

Agency and Impersonality

Their Linguistic and Cultural Manifestations

Mutsumi Yamamoto

Doshisha University

John Benjamins Publishing Company

Amsterdam / Philadelphia

Library of Congress Cataloging-in-Publication Data

Yamamoto, Mutsumi.
        Agency and impersonality : their linguistic and cultural manifestations /
            Mutsumi Yamamoto.
            p.   cm. (Studies in Language Companion Series, ISSN 0165–7763 ;
v. 78)
        Includes bibliographical references and index.
            1. Grammar, Comparative and general--Agent nouns. 2. Grammar,
        Comparative and general--Animacy. 3. Grammar, Comparative and
        general--Subjectless constructions. I. Title. II. Yamamoto, Mutsumi,
        1986-.

        P271.Y36 2006
        415--dc22   2006047728
        ISBN 90 272 3088 9 (Hb; alk. paper)

John Benjamins Publishing Co. · P.O. Box 36224 · 1020 ME Amsterdam · The Netherlands
John Benjamins North America · P.O. Box 27519 · Philadelphia PA 19118-0519 · USA

To Mija, the tortoise-shell cat

The poet's eye, in a fine frenzy rolling,
Doth glance from heaven to earth, from earth to heaven;
And, as imagination bodies forth
The forms of things unknown, the poet's pen
Turns them to shapes, and gives to airy nothing
A local habitation and a name.

(William Shakespeare, *A Midsummer Night's Dream*)

Table of contents

Acknowledgements

As always, I am in debt – and not in terms of money, but of gratitude. This book is the fruit of the research I undertook during my sabbatical leave at the University of Cambridge, which is one of my alma maters and filled with colourful and exciting memories. Firstly, I must thank my colleagues at Doshisha University, Kyoto, Japan, who gave me this wonderful opportunity of complete freedom. Chapters 1, 2 and 3 and the beginning of Chapter 4 were written in Cambridge, and the rest was completed back in Kyoto.

I am also indebted to my friends, colleagues and former teachers at the Universities of Cambridge, Lancaster and Oxford for their encouragement and constructive criticisms. Some kindly read and commented on the whole or parts of my manuscript, and some inspired me a great deal with their knowledge of linguistics, literature, philosophy and social anthropology, so much so that, from time to time, I had to make modifications even to the entire framework of the book. I am particularly grateful to Steven Bembridge, Jim Blevins, Gillian Brown, Roger Goodman, Jane Heal, Henrietté Hendrix, Mitsuyo Iwamoto, Geoffrey Leech and Ian Patterson.

Without the support and patience of Kees Vaes at John Benjamins Publishing Company, this book would not have seen the light of day. In particular, he kindly permitted me to use several important pieces of data that I have used in my previous book, *Animacy and Reference*, which is a sister volume of this book in the same series. I also appreciated his editorial assistance with the index, being a near computer idiot!

My heartfelt thanks go to 'Niu', who fed me well, helped me with computers and supported me under any circumstances – including the most strange ones. I also want to express my gratitude to my mother, Eriko, for feeding me well and staying well as ever.

M. Y.
Mt. Yoshida, Kyoto
November 2005

List of abbreviations

ABS	Absolutive
ACC	Accusative
AGT	Agentive
ASP	Aspect
AUX	Auxiliary
COP	Copula
DAT	Dative
ERG	Ergative
GEN	Genitive
HON	Honorific
IMP	Impersonal
LK	Linking particle
MASC	Masculine
NEG	Negative
NOM	Nominative
PART	Participle
PASS	Passive
PAST	Past
PAT	Patient
PERF	Perfective
PL	Plural
PREP	Preposition
PRES	Present
PROG	Progressive
QU	Question
SG	Singular
TAG	Tag question
TOP	Topic
TRANS	Transitive

CHAPTER 1

Introduction

A cat pouncing on a mouse is not really very different from you swatting a mosquito.

(Roger Caras, *A Cat is Watching*)

1.1 The importance of agency

The philosopher Donald Davidson defined the concept of 'agency' as follows: "a man is the agent of an act if what he does can be described under an aspect that makes it intentional" (1971:7). Certainly, as Davidson argues, human beings can be 'agents' – that is, we can intentionally initiate certain actions. By the same rationale, animals can be agents, too, as clearly demonstrated in the above citation from one of Roger Caras' books on cats, that was written out of the deep empathy towards the celebrated creatures shared by cat lovers all over the world, including myself.

It also seems to be the case that, sometimes to our regret, insects, such as cockroaches, can be perfect agents: they intentionally steal our food and, on their own initiative, run away from us in the most efficient possible way to save their own lives. Then, what about bacteria? Or can plants also be agents in quite a similar fashion as we – humans, animals and insects – can be agents?

Setting aside the scientific questions regarding the intentional behaviours of the so-called 'lower' animals and plants, one may metaphysically talk about creatures like scallops, as if they possess the same cognitive ability as ours and hence can behave in a very 'agentive' way as we humans do. For example, the Paris School sociologist Callon once described the difficulty in cultivating the scallops of St. Brieux Bay as follows:

(1) If the scallops are to be enrolled, they must first *be willing to anchor themselves to the collectors*. But this anchorage is not easy to achieve. In fact the researchers will have to lead their longest and most difficult negotiations with the scallops. (Callon 1986:211)

(2)   The researchers are ready to make any kind of concessions in order to lure the larvae into their trap. What sort of substances do larvae *prefer to anchor on*? Another series of transactions is necessary to answer the question.

(Callon 1986:213)

The expressions which are italicised in the above quotations, *be willing to anchor themselves to the collectors* and *prefer to anchor on*, clearly demonstrate the writer's attitude towards the issue in question: Callon treats (or pretends to treat) scallops as equal to human beings, presupposing their agency and intentionality. It is easy to imagine that the world begins to look like a different place, if we think of the scallops *who* act on their own will, when we find some of their dead bodies on a platter at a seafood restaurant. Of course, this example may be rather farfetched, but it certainly illustrates how strongly the agency concept may affect the way we observe and interpret the world that surrounds us.

This is not a book about scallops, but is an attempt to shed some light on the concept of 'agency', through observing its linguistic and cultural manifestations. A study on 'agency' on the basis of empirical research seems worthwhile, because it is a very important notion in explaining various aspects of human cognition and construction of ideas, and different ways of interpreting agency may, to a considerable extent, lead to different world-views. It can also be argued that agency is closely related to such notions as 'intentionality' and 'responsibility', to which we frequently appeal in our everyday life, particularly when something went wrong, and we need to place the blame for the unfortunate event onto somebody else. It follows then that the different ways in which we express and obfuscate agency would be most likely to result in different measures of accusing others and protecting ourselves.

It has been well recognised in the field of psychology that agency is one of the cognitively fundamental factors which constitute an important part of our epistemic attitudes towards the outside world. For instance, the cognitive model of schizophrenia, which has been advocated by Frith (1992), focuses upon the mechanisms involved in what is called 'agency disorders', as summarised in a set of three hypotheses by a French psychologist Pachoud (1999:214–215):

(3)   a.   An inability to carry out intentional actions may be a cause of impoverished action and speech observed in the negative form of schizophrenia.

b.   A planning disorder may account for the disorganisation of action and speech in schizophrenic patients, being exacerbated by the increase in automatic behaviour patterns, with certain environmental stimuli triggering motor routines. This could explain, among others, the 'distractible speech' of the schizophrenics, with sudden changes in discourse topic in response to irrelevant stimuli in the environment.

    c.   The third, more specific hypothesis aims at explaining 'agency disorders' as expressed by the patient feeling that he/she is not the initiator or subject of his/her own actions. This gives rise to pathological phenomena such as the experience of alien control where the patient has the impression of acting under the influence of outside forces and the phenomenon of thought insertion, involving a feeling of being dispossessed of one's own thoughts or a feeling of a loss of control over one's own thoughts.

Such 'agency disorders', Pachoud argues, can be caused by an impairment of the process known as 'motoring of action', through which individuals become aware of both their current action and their initiative to act, and by which they can exercise 'control' over the action; this mechanism can now be explained clearly by a neurophysiological theory of movement control (Pachoud 1999: 215). It is not my aim here to dive into the thorough account of such a neurophysiological theory, but the above argument on the 'agency disorders' as the central symptom of schizophrenia clearly demonstrates how essential the concept of agency is to human cognition. So much so that it is no wonder that philosophers have always tried to work out the systematised account of agency (and action) since Aristotle up to the present, as I will illustrate in Chapter 2.

The cognitive essentiality of agency naturally means that it is also a matter of significant interest in linguistics, since the same kind of opposition between its expression and obfuscation seems to be at work across a wide variety of languages on the Earth. Our cognition of agency and the extent to which we invest a certain entity (or a body of entities) with agency influence various levels of human language a great deal.

In the process of pinning down this 'enigmatic' notion of agency, it seems highly rewarding to examine a set of languages and cultures that demonstrates some fascinating examples of characteristic styles in encoding human agency. On the morpho-syntactic level, for example, a number of languages from different, unrelated language families are found to demonstrate 'agentive' system – as opposed to 'accusative' and 'ergative' systems – in which entities with an 'agentive' role in a sentence are explicitly marked as such (see, for instance, Dixon 1979; McLendon 1978; Palmer 1994; Van Valin 1985). One of the examples is the East Pomo language, a native American language in California, where the nature of the involvement of a particular entity in the action/event illustrated in a sentence is morphologically expressed as follows (McLendon 1978: 1–3):

(4)   *Xáꞏsꞏuꞏlàꞏ*   *wí*   *koꞏkʰóya.*
      Rattlesnake-AGT 1SG:PAT bit.
      'The rattlesnake bit me'.

(5) *Há*   *mí pal*   *šaˑkʼa.*
     1SG:AGT 3MASC:SG:PAT killed.
     'I killed him'.

(6) *Há*   *cʼe xélka.*
     1SG:AGT slip.
     'I am sliding'.

(7) *Wí*   *cʼe xélka.*
     1SG:PAT slip.
     'I am slipping'.

In the sentences (4) to (7), 'AGT' and 'PAT' indicate the morphological distinction of 'agentive' and 'patientive', which can be regarded as case markers like 'nominative', 'accusative' or 'ergative', 'absolutive'. Such languages or systems are called 'agentive' (Palmer 1994: 14).

The examples such as above certainly illustrate the pervasive influence of the agency concept on the structure of languages. However, the main focus of the current book is upon the semantic, pragmatic and, where necessary, sociolinguistic aspects of language, rather than its syntactic and morphological aspects, since different world-views can be more clearly observed through different modes of language use and of encoding of meaning than through different morpho-syntactic rules.

For this reason, throughout the course of this book, I will be concentrating on the two languages, Japanese and English, which exhibit strikingly different tendencies towards the semantic, pragmatic and sociolinguistic manifestations of 'agency'. (Accidentally, their birthplaces, too, are located at the eastern and western ends of Eurasia.) Together with the linguistic expression of agency, I will also investigate some relevant cultural values into which the surface linguistic manifestations are deeply rooted.

The simple examples in (8) and (9) below would be sufficient to highlight the distinct styles of conceptualisation of human agency commonly found in Japanese and English:

(8) *Nichiyōbi heiten.*
     Sunday   closed:shop.

(9) We are closed on Sundays.   (Ikegami 1982: 90)

The above examples are typical messages in the two languages in question letting the customers know that the shop is closed on Sundays. The Japanese expression in (8) has no human subject; it is not clear at all who is instigating an intentional action of closing the shop. On the other hand, by means of the subject *we*, the corresponding English sentence saliently expresses the people – the proprietor and/or the shop attendants – who are responsible for closing this shop on Sundays.

As will be discussed in further details in the later chapters of this book, this difference in encoding the human entities between Japanese and English seems to (at least partially) stem from their style of expressing (and not expressing) human 'agency', and the expression and suppression of agency in these languages clearly reflect the essential part of the particular 'mind-styles' that are shared by their speakers. Of course, it must be borne in mind, at the outset, that Japanese is by no means the only language which makes a sharp contrast with English in terms of the encoding of 'agency'; it has been reported that a number of other languages from unrelated language families, such as Irish and Hopi, exhibit similar tendencies to that of Japanese (cf. Hartmann 1954; Whorf 1956; Ikegami 1982).

The term 'mind-style', as Roger Fowler coins it, means 'any distinctive linguistic presentation of an individual mental self' (Fowler 1977:103). In many cases, as Fowler maintains, this can display an individual's 'preoccupations', 'prejudices', 'perspectives' and 'values', which strongly bias one's world-view, but of which he or she may be quite unaware. It naturally follows, then, that there is an inevitable need to discuss the relativistic view on the interrelationship between language, thought and culture, which has been revisited in the current intellectual climate but from renewed perspectives.

The original idea of linguistic relativity, which is attributable to Humboldt, Boas, Sapir and Whorf, was that "the semantic structures of different languages might be fundamentally incommensurable, with the consequences for the way in which speakers of specific languages might think and act" (Gumperz & Levinson 1996:2). In this tradition, particular emphasis was placed on the point that the grammatical system in each natural language determines the way in which its speakers would dissect, interpret and explain the outside world. Below is one of the famous remarks made by Whorf:

(10)   It is the grammatical background of our mother tongue, which includes not only our way of constructing propositions but the way we dissect nature and break up the flux of experience into objects and entities to construct propositions about.
(Whorf 1956:239)

It can be argued, in a nutshell, that the deterministic tone of the above quotation could be one of the major factors which triggered the swing of the pendulum – the so-called 'Sapir-Whorf hypothesis' has long been labelled as rather extreme under the influence of deductive and rationalistic assumption held by the generative linguists.[1] However, despite the recent scepticism, there are indeed many actual observations of language-specific effect on human cognitive processing (cf. Gumperz & Levinson 1996; Lucy 1992b; Nuyts & Pederson 1997, *inter alia*), some striking examples of which will be reviewed in a later chapter.

One small case to illustrate this interrelation is, of course, the above mentioned contrast between the English and Japanese ways of encoding the fact that the shop is closed on Sundays. However, it must be noted that the different manifestations of human entities in the examples in (8) and (9) do not only stem from the difference in syntactic structures – upon which the central focus fell in Whorf's arguments – but are largely concerned with, as I have argued, the difference in semantic, pragmatic and socio-cultural connotation of 'agency' between the two languages.

One of the recent changes in the interpretation of the Whorfian hypothesis is that, as Lucy (1992a: 178) points out, linguistic relativity – at least in Whorf's version – does not rule out the possibility of discovering semantic universals. This point, however, implies at the same time yet another possibility of discovering semantic relativity and, further, pragmatic relativity and sociolinguistic relativity (cf. Yamamoto 2000), along with syntactic relativity as traditionally presupposed. Recognising different levels of universality and relativity will then turn out to be particularly important in my later discussions on the linguistic manifestations of 'agency'.

In connection with the above arguments on linguistic relativity, a brief remark on Franz Boas' concept of 'cultural relativism' may well be made here (Boas 1911): the concept of relativity is naturally applicable to various facets of the societies and cultures which embrace languages themselves. Whilst Boas was transcribing and translating native American texts, he came to acquire the view that each individual culture of Amerindians should be understood in its own terms rather than as a part of an intellectually scaled master plan in which 'familiar languages of Europe' occupy dominant positions. This idea is what is called 'cultural relativism', and it originated from the awareness of different modes classifying the world and human experience in miscellaneous languages of America (Duranti 1997: 54).

Given that, for instance, the difference between the ways in which the Japanese and English languages encode human agency is 'incommensurable', what does this mean from a point of view of linguistic and (socio-)cultural relativism? To answer this question, we need to observe the patterns of the 'mind-styles' shared by the speakers of these two languages and certain cultural values which underlie the specific ways they would think and act. By the end of this book, it will be hopefully proven that 'enigmas of agency' can indeed explicate not only the differences in surface linguistic expressions, but also some notable variations of 'world-views', mainly through both quantitative and qualitative research into the linguistic (and cultural) manifestations of agency in Japanese and English.

1.2 The structure of this book

The aim of the following chapter is to try to establish the conceptual framework of 'agency'. Our first concern will be Aristotle's discussion on the opposition between

the primacy of 'object' and that of 'action'. The arguments by the modern philosophers, such as Donald Davidson and Irving Thalberg, constitute a good part of the
conceptual framework that will be employed for the rest of this book. We will then
embark upon the epistemological salience of the agency concept, studying first the
hypothetical language of a Neanderthal man (who is of course (!) an imaginary
character created by the novelist William Golding) as an antithesis, and then examining the degree of contribution of agency towards the notion of 'mind-style',
advocated by Fowler.

The cognitive salience of agency also means that, by manipulating the expression of agency, one can manipulate the way the others would think and act; the
political significance of agency (and its use and misuse) will also be one of the
foci in Chapter 2. The last section of Chapter 2 will be solely devoted for eluci-
dating the relationship between the agency concept and that of 'animacy', which
has always been closely associated with agency. This will again reveal some intriguing aspects of the notion of agency which will explicate the very core of its
'enigma', particularly its strong influence on the way we recognise, dissect and
explain the world.

The first part of Chapter 3 will be focussed on the linguistic application of
the agency concept, particularly, in the field of syntax and semantics. The characterisation of agency by linguists has always had recourse to the scale of 'semantic
roles', that extends from 'Agent', 'Experiencer' and 'Beneficiary', through 'Instrument', 'Patient', etc. to rather peripheral constituents of a clause, such as 'Location'
and 'Time'. We will mainly review the terminological arguments with a particular focus on the works of the Case Grammarians (cf., for instance, Fillmore 1968,
1971; Chafe 1970; Cook 1989) and the Functional Linguists (such as Dik 1978,
1989; Siewierska 1991).

The grammatical 'machinery' which we adopt will be the Functional Grammarians' definition of agency and semantic roles including that of 'Agent', which
is congenial to our philosophical arguments in Chapter 2, particularly in terms of
the treatment of animacy and intentionality. The linguistic framework *a la* Simon
Dik will be employed when the actual manifestations of agency in Japanese and
English will be investigated.

To demonstrate how differently the agency concept can be manifested in human language, the extremely impersonal and 'de-agentivised' expression of agency
in Japanese will be contrasted to the highly articulated manifestation of human
agentivity in English. When exploring the linguistic manifestations of agency, use
will be made of the relatively small parallel Japanese and English corpus, yielding
salient statistical discussions that demonstrate the clear-cut opposition between
the obfuscation and the articulation of agency in the two languages. A particular
attention will be directed to the 'impersonality' phenomena concerning the ex-

pression of agency in Japanese, which will be analysed primarily as a large-scale grammatical feature of this language.

In Chapter 4, we will go beyond the syntactic confines of the Functionalists' definition of agency and will embark upon the further interpretation of the opposition between its obfuscation and articulation, in search for the semantic, pragmatic and socio-cultural motives facilitating the particular patterns of encoding agency in Japanese and English. Along with the cases which will have been observed within the Functional Grammarians' framework in Chapter 3, those cases illustrating the less obvious manifestations of agency, that cannot be explained in terms of the semantic role of 'Agent', will also be taken into account here.

Again, one of our main foci will be upon the suppression of agency or the expression of 'impersonality' in Japanese; a variety of measures of impersonalising human entities will be studied from pragmatic and socio-cultural perspectives. In Chapter 4, the contrastive ways of treating human agency in Japanese and English will be ascribed to the different 'mind-styles' or 'world-views' and further to the different cultural and behavioural norms, that are prevalently reflected in these languages. This means that we need to have recourse to 'linguistic relativism' regarding the interrelationship between 'language', 'thought' and 'culture', not in pursuit of a 'deterministic' idea about one's native language dominating one's thought, but in an attempt to elucidate the 'chicken-and-egg' dilemma concerning which influences which. A brief remark on the historical background of 'Sapir-Whorf hypothesis' has been given earlier in this chapter, but we will re-examine in more detail what Benjamin Whorf termed as the 'linguistic relativity principle',[2] in comparison with its recent reincarnation, 'neo-Whorfianism' (Levinson 2003). Finally, in the last section of Chapter 4, the theoretical discussions on linguistic (and socio-cultural) relativity will be brought into practice as a means of explaining the Japanese and English styles of treating agency, with supplementary socio-cultural facts that throw some light upon the 'collectivistic' view on agency in Japanese society.

The fifth (and last) chapter will address some 'enigmas' concerning agency and impersonality, which will not have been covered in the main arguments in Chapters 2, 3 and 4. These will fall into several different domains. One of such issues will be the contrast between 'agentive' and 'impersonal' rhetoric: some interesting examples of literary texts in the English and Japanese languages will be considered in order to explore strikingly different 'mind-styles' concerning 'personification' or what has been termed as 'pathetic fallacy'. Another issue of note will be concerned solely with the realm of the impersonality concept. Impersonal construction of clauses can be found quite widely in languages over the world, and there can be a possibility that some common denominators may be found across a variety of linguistic stocks, including Japanese of course. In this concluding (but not conclusive) chapter, it will be pointed out that all our discussions so far have been upon the different fashions of dissecting the 'world', and that reference has to be made to the very nature of what is called 'reality', which Albert Einstein characterised as a 'paradox' exclusively composed of 'fancies'.

CHAPTER 2

What is agency?

The dead tree by Lok's ear acquired a voice.
"Clop!"

(William Golding, The Inheritors)

2.1 Overview

When you read the above lines from William Golding's *The Inheritors*, what kind of impression does it make on your mind? For instance, you may be puzzled and wonder: 'What does a "dead tree" mean?' or 'How does it "acquire" a voice?'

This is not exactly a piece of nonsensical writing, however absurd it may appear. Once the context surrounding this particular text is revealed, one will begin to appreciate that it is actually meant to be a depiction of a world which is quite remote from the one in which we live ourselves. Lok is a Neanderthal man. The tree is 'dead', because Lok's enemy who is more technologically advanced has just shot an arrow at it. 'Clop' is the sound that the arrow made, when it hit the tree beside Lok.

The Inheritors is a novel which deals with the prehistoric battle between Neanderthal man and *Homo sapiens* or 'the new people', the natural consequence being that the latter conquer the former, whose intelligence is supposed to be considerably inferior. Golding's special effect to demonstrate this intellectual inferiority of the Neanderthal was that he did not grant his Neanderthal characters the ability to fully understand human 'agency'. A tree may 'acquire a voice' in the world where one cannot sense properly the agency of another human being who shoots an arrow at it. Golding's imaginary world with distorted agency will be discussed in more depth in a later section, but it can be argued here that the distorted description of agency goes against our 'commonsense' view of the world; this is why we would feel somewhat uneasy or intrigued when pressed to imagine a 'dead tree' which 'acquires a voice'. At least a part of the 'enigma' of agency lies in the point that it may be highly illusory, when encoded in a particular way by means of our language.

What is the source of this illusion created by agency? How can we utilise or abuse such illusive effects of agency? How have the philosophers been trying to reveal the secret of this intriguing notion of agency? These are some of the basic questions which will be addressed in this chapter.

At the very beginning of Chapter 1, I introduced the definition of the agency concept by the philosopher Donald Davidson, which goes "a man is the agent of an act if what he does can be described under an aspect that makes it intentional" (1971: 7), as though it is self-evident. However, this definition needs further explanations, and, in establishing the general framework of agency, a more thorough anatomy of the concept is indispensable. In the following section, we will explore the philosophical background of our starting point, i.e. the question: 'What is agency?', casting our mind back to the antiquity.

We will then come back to the Lok's world to consider further the conceptual salience of agency in our cognition in Section 2.3. Section 2.4 will focus upon the manipulation of agency in the use of our language, which is one of the most eminent reasons why I have argued that the agency concept can be 'highly illusory'.

In Section 2.5, our theme will be the correlation between agency and the concept of 'animacy', which has been traditionally associated with that of agency from the Greek antiquity (see, for example, Aristotle's *De Anima*) up to the present. In a nutshell, animacy can be regarded as some kind of assumed cognitive scale extending from human through animal to inanimate (Yamamoto 1999: 1), and, again in a nutshell, its correlation between agency is: being an agent presupposes being an animate being, who/which is sentient, that is, who/which possesses a soul or 'animator' (in Aristotle's terms, *psuchê*).

2.2 'Intentionality' and some satellite concepts: Philosophical discussions

What is 'agency'? The aim of this section is to try to partially answer this fathomless question, mainly by reviewing various opinions of philosophers, both ancient and contemporary, and focussing on the relation between agency and its associated concepts.

To begin with, casting our mind back to the Greek antiquity, let us think about the case of Oedipus' getting married to his mother as dramatised in Sophocles' tragedy, *Oedipus Tyrannus*. Of course, it was only unintentionally that Oedipus married his mother; however, at the same time, his marrying the woman Jocasta is the result of his conscious drive. Is Oedipus an 'agent' at all under these circumstances? Some argue that the answer must definitely be 'yes', but from a less rigorous point of view, it can be both 'yes' and 'no' simultaneously, with two separate events involved.

Answering the above question concerning Oedipus' 'agentive' marriage requires the fundamental deconstruction of the agency concept itself. One of the simplest and clearest is that of Donald Davidson (1971:7), which we envisaged in Chapter 1 (and just above):

(1) ... a man is the agent of an act if what he does can be described under an aspect that makes it intentional.

The very core of Davidson's definition is that the agency concept is presupposed by that of 'intentionality'.[1] Davidson also argues that there can be a fairly definite subclass of 'events' which are 'actions', and that it can be achieved by appeal to the concept of intention. "If an event is an action", then "under some description(s) it is intentional" (Davidson 1971:25). According to Davidson's theory, Oedipus' marrying to his mother (or Jocasta) is to be labelled as an action, but my waking up this morning is not. 'Waking up' is not an action, because it cannot be attributed intentionality under normal circumstances, whereas Oedipus' marrying Jocasta is intentional 'under some description'.

However, we have to be a little careful when handling the expression 'under an aspect' or 'under some description(s)' in the above mentioned characterisations of agency by Davidson. For example, even when there is an unintentional incident, such as Oedipus' marrying his mother, that is only because there is an identical event which is an action he performed intentionally, namely, marrying Jocasta. In such a case, following the Davidsonian argument, it is plausible to argue that Oedipus' marriage to his mother is intentional in that he intentionally married Jocasta, who happened to be his mother; since one aspect of his marriage involves intentionality, Oedipus is the 'agent' of this 'action'.

Davidson argues that certain kinds of mistake make particularly interesting examples to illustrate the relationship between agency and intentionality. Misreading a sign, misinterpreting an order, underestimating a weight or miscalculating a sum – these errors cannot be made intentionally under normal circumstances (cf. Davidson 1971:6). Of course, we must disregard instances such as someone in a weight watchers course always underestimating his or her weight. To make a genuine mistake of one of the above mentioned kinds is to fail to do what one intends, and, as Davidson construes, no one can intend to fail. Nevertheless, these mistakes are 'actions', and those who make them are 'agents', because "making a mistake must in each case be doing something else intentionally" (Davidson 1971:6).

An interesting borderline case[2] is provided by another contemporary philosopher, Chisholm (1966:37). Suppose that Bill intends to kill his uncle. Suppose he is thinking about how he is going to kill his uncle while driving, and suppose his intention to kill his uncle makes him so nervous and excited that he suddenly hits and kills a pedestrian who happens to be his uncle. It is the case that Bill killed his uncle and that his intention to kill his uncle was one of the causes of his killing his uncle. However, this is an accident. It is impossible to claim that Bill killed his uncle intentionally; that is, he is not the agent of killing his uncle. Instead, what this man was doing intentionally must have been something like 'driving home safely'. This means (from a Davidsonian perspective) that, ironically enough, Bill is still an agent of 'driving home safely', but not that of 'killing his uncle'.

Along with Davidson, John R. Searle (1983:82) also categorically claims: "there are no actions without intentions", but at a later stage he becomes somewhat softened and states: "... there are *in general* no actions without corresponding intentions". Searle's chief purpose here is to show the contrast between 'intention' on one hand and such concepts as 'belief' and 'desire' on the other hand; there are many states of affairs without corresponding beliefs and many states of affairs without corresponding desires in contrast to the cases of actions with corresponding intentions.[3]

Then how can we pursue yet another possibility, that is, Oedipus can be an agent and a non-agent at the same time in the event of marrying his mother? It is interesting to realise that the foundation for our current arguments on the features of agency has already been laid by the ancient scientist philosopher, Aristotle, who was also a literary critic and analysed the rhetorical characteristics of Sophocles' tragedy *Oedipus Tyrannus*[4] himself. He addressed exactly the same problem as discussed above in *Nicomachean Ethics* (*Common Books*), but using a different example.

Merope kills a man who approached her, and, by doing so, she kills her son. According to Aristotle, Merope kills her son unintentionally and yet kills a man intentionally; in doing so, she would perform two distinct actions: one intentional, the other unintentional. He further maintains that the sentences "Merope killed her son" and "Merope killed the man who approached" describe different actions (Charles 1984:63). Applying the Davidsonian definition of agency as presupposing intentionality to the Aristotelian analysis of 'twofold' intentionality, we can possibly argue that Merope (and Oedipus, too) is an agent and a non-agent of killing her son (of marrying his mother, in the case of Oedipus) at the same time.

It is worth examining the classification of 'actions' by Aristotle here following Charles (1984:104–105). Aristotle discerns a variety of cases which he treats separately:

(2) a. non-self-moved processes, e.g. growing old, breathing
     b. sub-intentional processes which are self-moved, e.g. frowning, sexually aroused
     c. intentional processes, not supported by practical reasoning
     d. intentional processes supported by practical reasoning
     e. intentional states: remaining at one's post

Amongst the five categories in (2), Aristotle is prepared to treat (2a–d) as 'actions' (*Nicomachean Ethics* (*Common Books*)), even though (2a) and (2b) need not be intentional under any description. Further, as Charles (1984:105) points out, it is interesting to note that he did not "seek to force all actions and relevant inactions into one procrustean framework of processes which are intentional under some description". By this rationale, both Oedipus marrying his mother and Merope killing her son are to be regarded as 'agents' anyway, whether or not they performed their actions intentionally.

There are two more points to be made out of the above taxonomical argument by Aristotle. Firstly, Aristotle (and his interpreter, Charles) recognise(s) that the categories of (2c) and (2d), which are both 'intentional', are the 'central cases of agency' (Charles 1984:105). This suggests that Aristotle seems to treat 'intention' as a factor which constitutes the core of the concept of 'agency'. In fact, Aristotle proposes separate criteria in an attempt to characterise 'intentional actions' as an important, independent notion in terms of 'causation' and 'knowledge'. He argues that z is a voluntary (or an intentional)[5] action of S's at $t1$ iff: (1) z is a bodily movement of S's at $t1$; (2) S knows the relevant particulars involved in doing z (what he is doing at $t1$; to whom; with what); and (3) z is an action which is caused either by S's desire to do a z-type action (for itself or derivatively) *or* by his desire to do a y-type action (for itself or derivatively), when S knows that in doing y he is also doing z (Charles 1984:58–61).

After all, the relationship between agency and intentionality is to be interpreted as an inseparable one, but the extent to which it should be stressed can be a matter of degree or gradience; as George Lakoff argues, intentionality (or volition)[6] is one of the properties of 'prototypical agency' along with such a property as primary responsibility for action (Lakoff 1987:66). In the current project, I will basically adhere to Davidson's definition of agency as cited in (1) above for the sake of simplicity, but, at the same time, I would like to suggest the importance of being flexible from time to time, taking into account the Aristotelian insights and the 'prototypical' view of agency.

The second point to note regarding Aristotle's classification of actions shown in the citation (2) is that it seems to be based on (or at least, closely related to) his hierarchical view of the natural world; this is of particular interest in relation to what is called 'animacy hierarchy', which will be further explored in Section 2.5.

According to Barnes (2000), Everson (1995) and many others, the concept of *psuchê*, which is usually – but quite misleadingly – translated as 'soul', is always in the centre of Aristotle's psychological writings. Since Aristotle regards *psuchê* (from which 'psychology' and other related words derive) as to be possessed by all living things – daffodils, scallops and squirrels no less than human beings and gods, its better English translation can be something like 'animator' (Barnes 2000:105). From a commonsense point of view, it may be slightly odd to attribute 'soul' to such creatures as daffodils and scallops, but it sounds more natural to say that plants and other so-called 'lower' animals possess an 'animator', which animates or gives life to a living thing.

In *De Anima*, Aristotle argues that different creatures are endowed with *psuchai* (plural form of *psuchê*) or animators of different complexity:

(3)   Some things possess all the powers of the animator, others some of them, others one only. The powers we mentioned were those of nutrition, of perception, of appetition, of change in place, of thought. Plants possess only the nutritive power. Other things possess both that and the power of perception. And if the power of perception, then that of appetition too. For appetition consists of desire, inclination and wish; all animals possess at least one of the senses, namely touch; everything which has perception also experiences pleasure and pain, the pleasant and the painful; and everything which experiences those also possesses desire (for desire is appetition for the pleasant) ... Some things possess in addition to these the power of locomotion; and others also possess the power of thought and intelligence.[7]

On the basis of his taxonomy of nature, Aristotle assumes that certain creatures are naturally marked out in virtue of enjoying consciousness and intentionality (Everson 1995: 168). His hierarchical view of *psuchê* or 'animator' and its capacities presupposes his hierarchical taxonomy of living things (including gods!) that populate the world and, to a considerable extent, corresponds to his classification of actions (as shown in the quotation (2)), which are typically performed by living creatures of certain stature.

For example, plants can doubtless perform the 'actions' of type (2a), that is, non-self-moved processes, but, from a commonsense view of the world, it seems highly unlikely that they can perform the actions of types (2b), sub-intentional processes which are self-moved, (2c), intentional processes not supported by practical reasoning, and (2d), intentional processes supported by reasoning. However, we can also think of a case in which insectivorous plants skilfully snap at a little fly at the very right moment, calculating the exact timing. Aren't they performing a very careful, intentional action supported by reasoning?

Anyhow, setting aside such farfetched examples, the action types (2c) and (2d) are labelled as the most 'central' or 'prototypical' cases of agency, and they are presupposed by 'intentionality', as the contemporary philosophers such as Davidson and Searle claim. An important implication here is that the 'higher' action types, as illustrated by Aristotle as in (2c) and (2d), can be naturally associated with the typical behaviours of higher animals (or highly anthropomorphised animals), human beings and supernatural beings like gods. It follows then that the 'central cases of agency', underlaid with intentionality, prototypically belong to the realms of higher animals, humans and gods.

Our discussions on the 'chain' of natural beings, the construction of their *psuchai* and their typical actions may go on forever. We shall now turn to the philosophical features of some other relevant concepts which have been traditionally associated with that of agency, but not quite as strongly as intentionality: namely, awareness (knowledge) of action, causation (or causality) and responsibility.

In the first instance, let us begin with the notion of awareness of action. A contemporary linguist Mimi Klaiman proposes another way of deconstructing the agency concept, arguing that agency presupposes both (1) animacy and (2) awareness of the action (1991:113). For the moment, we will only focus upon (2) awareness of the action, leaving behind (1) animacy until we come back to it in Section 2.5.

'Awareness of the action', which Klaiman regards as a necessary component in characterising the agency concept, may remind the readers of Aristotle's account of intentional (or voluntary) actions which we examined in the preceding discussion. Attention is to be paid to the same passage again, but this time our focus will be upon the second condition which satisfies a part of his characterisation of voluntary or intentional actions.

As argued above, Aristotle argues that z is a voluntary (or an intentional) action of S's at $t1$ iff: (1) z is a bodily movement of S's at $t1$; (2) S knows the relevant particulars involved in doing z (what he is doing at $t1$; to whom; with what); and (3) z is an action which is caused either by S's desire to do a z-type action (for itself or derivatively) *or* by his desire to do a y-type action (for itself or derivatively), when S knows that in doing y he is also doing z (Charles 1984:58–61). One point has to be made supplementarily here: since Aristotle – unlike Davidson and Searle – does not regard all actions as intentional, he has to specifically limit his discussion only to the actions which are intentional or voluntary.

Aristotle's point here seems more concrete than the expression 'awareness of the action': he specifically states that one has to know what he/she is performing, who or what is/are to be affected by the action, what instrument(s) is/are required to perform the action. When taking into account a part of the third condition above, one has to even 'know' the teleological effect of his/her action. Whether the 'knowledge' of such minute details of the relevant particulars involved in an action is a necessary condition of performing an intentional action (or simply, an action, following Davidson and Searle) is a question we will not ask ourselves in the current context, but it is reasonable to state here that the concept of 'awareness' or 'knowledge' is a relevant factor in characterising the overall nature of agency.

Derivatively, the notion of 'control' has also been traditionally associated with that of 'awareness of action' and 'intentionality'. Irving Thalberg's (1972:66) following statement seems quite adequate to illustrate the relevance of the 'control' concept to those of 'awareness', 'intentionality' and 'agency' itself:

(4)   But more important is the extra-linguistic tie between awareness and control. Normally, the episodes we count as a person's intentional actions, and hence

as being under his control, are also events of which he is aware – often without observation.

The notion of 'control' will prove to be particularly useful in the following section, where the behaviours of Lok the Neanderthal will be analysed in terms of his faculty of controlling the physical world.

'Causation' or 'causality' is our next subject, but we must be more cautious here since there have been many conflicting opinions about it in its relation to agency. In the above mentioned argument on intentional/voluntary actions by Aristotle, it is also quite noticeable that Aristotle analyses voluntary or intentional action in terms of both 'knowledge' and 'causality' (or 'causation'). Under the third condition which constitutes a part of Aristotle's characterisation of voluntary/intentional actions, he clearly argues that the agent's causation of the event in question (or, more specifically, the agent's desire causing the relevant event) is a necessary component of an intentional action.

As far as the involvement of causation/causality in the characterisation of agency is concerned, modern philosophers have aired a number of doubts. For example, Davidson has shown the limitation to purely causal analysis (Charles 1984: 59), maintaining that the notion of 'cause' has nothing directly to do with the relation between an agent and an action (Davidson 1971: 25). Thalberg (1972: 17–18) also attacks 'the old-fashioned analysis along causal-lines', particularly that of David Hume,[8] which goes like this: we bring about our overt behaviour by doing something else first *in foro interno*. According to Hume, we engage in an act of willing before performing the action itself. In the case of Aristotle, it is desiring that precedes the process of the actual performance of voluntary/intentional action itself. Thalberg's (1972) main argument is that an agent causes his/her action just through performing the relevant action itself, not by doing anything else beforehand. Therefore, as far as the relationship between agency and the causation/causality concept is concerned, I will try to keep it outside the scope of our discussions, except when it is absolutely necessary to mention it. Modern linguists too are split into two camps as to the treatment of causation as a potential component of agency: for instance, whilst Talmy (2000: 509–542) regards agency as an aspect of the semantics of causation, Hundt (2004: 49) considers such process-internal analysis of the relationship between agency and causation as in Talmy's argument to be irrelevant to her analysis of the agency concept.

The 'responsibility'[9] concept is also deeply intertwined to that of agency, and the relationship between them is quite straightforward and does not seem to require as much caution as in the case of causality. As argued by George Lakoff, a student of prototype theory would readily claim that amongst the agent properties are such factors as 'primary responsibility for the action' and volition or intentionality (Lakoff 1987; Van Oosten 1984).

Davidson (1971:9) construes that, whereas attributions of intention are basically concerned with excuses and justifications, attributions of agency are typically accusations or assignments of responsibility. This point highlights the importance of the agency concept in our everyday life; we frequently appeal to it, particularly when something went wrong, and we need to place the blame for the unfortunate event onto somebody else. The different ways in which we express and obfuscate agency would be most likely to result in different measures of accusing the others and protecting ourselves, and this is where the potentially 'face threatening' nature of the agency concept lies. In Section 2.4, we will be focussing on the problem of how the attributions of agency and responsibility can be interpreted in our actual use of language.

Now that a series of philosophical discussions made clear the conceptual basis of agency in relation to its 'satellite concepts', such as intentionality, awareness of action, control, causality and responsibility, we will then revisit the episode of Lok the Neanderthal, with which the curtain of the current chapter rose. In the following section, 'the Lok language' will be re-examined on the ground of the general characterisation of agency provided above; a focus of our argument will be placed on the cognitive salience of agency and its contribution to the formation of a particular world-view.

2.3 Cognitive salience and 'mind-style'

First of all, let us remind ourselves of the definition of the concept of 'mind-style'. As outlined in Chapter 1, Roger Fowler (1977:103) characterises this term as 'any distinctive linguistic representation of an individual mental self'. He maintains that, above all, 'mind-style' can display preoccupations, prejudices, perspectives and values which may bias an individual's 'world-view', but of which he or she may quite likely be unconscious. Fowler's chief interest is to apply this notion to literary criticism, particularly the analysis of novels, but it is also useful in characterising the mental state of real living human beings. In this book, we will make use of the 'mind-style' concept in analysing the 'world-view' or the 'mental self' of both fictional characters inside fictions and real life human beings including the authors of fictions.

Having established the general philosophical framework of agency and reintroduced the term 'mind-style', we are fully in a position to discuss the language of Lok, an imaginary Neanderthal man, to illustrate the salient position which 'agency' occupies in our cognition. Below is the passage which includes the lines quoted at the beginning of this chapter:

(5)   The bushes twitched again. Lok steadied by the tree and gazed. A head
and a chest faced him, half-hidden. There were white bone things behind the
leaves and the hair. The man had white bone things above his eyes and under
the mouth so that his face was longer than a face should be. The man turned
sideways in the bushes and looked at Lok along his shoulder. A stick rose
upright and there was a lump of bone in the middle. Lok peered at the stick
and the lump of bone and the small eyes in the bone things over the face.
Suddenly Lok understood that the man was holding a stick out to him but
neither he nor Lok could reach across the river. He would have laughed if it
were not for the echo of the screaming in his head. The stick began to grow
shorter at both ends. Then it shot out to full length again.

   The dead tree by Lok's ear acquired a voice.
   "Clop!"
   His ear twitched and he turned to the tree.

(William Golding, *The Inheritors*)

As outlined at the beginning of the current chapter, the novelist tries to demonstrate the intellectual crudeness of the Neanderthal by not granting Lok the
faculty of comprehending agency. That is why, in Lok's world, the 'dead tree'
'acquires a voice'.

M. A. K. Halliday (1971) analyses Golding's characteristic style of writing in
The Inheritors, pointing out that, although the language describes Lok perceiving
a sequence of 'actions', those 'actions' are perceived in such a way that reveals the
weakness of the human entities' 'control' over the activity taking place in the world
around them. "The picture is one in which people act, but they do not act on
things; they move, but they move only themselves, not other objects" (Halliday
1971: 349). Fowler further elaborates the above interpretation of the Lok language
by Halliday and argues that Lok's (potential) world-view is the one "which might
have been held by pre-technological man, man innocent of his innate ability to
manipulate his environment and other human beings" (1977: 105).

Scientifically speaking, the credibility of Golding's view on the epistemic attitudes of Neanderthal men may be quite low. How could the prehistoric hunters
survive, if they were unable to read correctly the intentionality and agency of their
preys? In the field of development psychology, it has been testified that children
acquire the ability of distinguishing the sentient from the insentient at a very
early stage, the notion of sentiency naturally incorporating those of intentionality, awareness of action, etc. Using a criterion of 83% correct responses (5 out of 6,
or 10 out of 12 correct), Tunmer found that 22 4- and 5-year-old children (out of
his 24 subjects) reached the criterion of the recognition of unacceptable sentences
involving sentient/non-sentient (or animate/inanimate) distinction (1985: 995).

Setting aside the scientific fact, in the world of fictions at least, we can often observe a certain correlation between the 'mind-style' of a particular character in question and his or her (or the author's) favourite syntactic patterns in which the character's thoughts are revealed in overwhelmingly a majority of cases. Halliday maintains that, in the first nine-tenths of Golding's *The Inheritors*, where the world is observed through Lok's eyes, the typically Neanderthal perception is conveyed by a choice of some basic syntactic structures and avoidance of others. Particularly, according to Halliday's observation, a lack of transitive clauses (Subject + Verb + Object) with human subjects is conspicuous.

What does this imply? In Lok's universe, "The bushes twitched again"; it seems quite inappropriate to express the same situation as in "Lok's enemy rustled the bushes again" in a transitive clause accompanied by a human subject. It is not a human agent who has a power to change his/her environment, but an inanimate object is expressed as though it can move of its own accord when it has actually been shifted by a person (Halliday 1971; Fowler 1977). This distinction between animate beings and inanimate objects is a very important one to characterise a significant facet of 'agency' and will be discussed with a greater depth in Section 2.5.

In (6) is a list of some other 'events' which took place in the above citation, as they are originally expressed by Golding:

(6)   a.   A stick rose upright.
      b.   The stick began to grow shorter at both ends.
      c.   The dead tree by Lok's ear acquired the voice.

These certainly sound quite differently from the 'actions'[10] expressed by transitive clauses as in (7) below, that can carry the same information, but with a dash of much stronger human agency and intentionality:

(7)   a.   The enemy lifted the bow upright.
      b.   He drew the bow.
      c.   He shot an arrow at the tree beside Lok with a screaming sound.

Examining a little longer piece of the text than that in (5), Halliday further maintains that a human being is sometimes expressed either in terms of parts of his body or as inanimate objects (as in "A head and a chest faced him, half-hidden"), and that, of the human subjects, half are found in clauses which are not clauses of 'action' (1971:349). Indeed, in the Lok language, the agent is seldom a human being (Halliday 1971:353). Lok's 'limited' epistemic attitude, which does not allow him to distinguish the agentive from non-agentive objects, significantly characterises his 'mind-style' (cf. Fowler 1977:106). In the distorted world with wrongly perceived agency, people and bushes seem to share the same ontological status and faculty of intentionality; this suggests, with no doubt, that the perception of agency greatly affects our view of the whole world.

After pondering about what primitive human epistemic attitude could be, it may be of some interest to think about (or simply imagine!) what this world may look like when observed by someone who is far more intelligent than *Homo sapiens*. Below is an extract from William Kotzwinkle's novel, *E.T.*, based on a motion picture by Melissa Mathison, which shows clearly that 'agency' is a key concept in characterising the protagonist's mind-style or world-view:

(8)   But the communicator was nearly complete.

"Yeah," said Michael, "but what's gonna run it? What's gonna turn *this*?" He spun the saw blade on the turntable. "If we take it up in the hills there" – he pointed out the window – "there won't be any electricity."

The space-being had just completed supper. Torch-fingering his butter knife, he took out the temper, then bent and bolted it to the coat hanger, along with the fork, to form a ratchet device: knife and fork moved in and out of the teeth of the saw blade, advancing it tooth by tooth.

"Yeah," said Michael, "but we can't stand out there all night, yanking that thing around."

The extraterrestrial continued smiling. He understood it all now, those early hints flashed at him from within, of a little fork dancing around a plate. It was this thing he'd made, and it would work, out in the hills, and no hands, human or otherwise, would be needed to activate it.

(William Kotzwinkle, *E.T.*)

The extraterrestrial, left alone on the Earth, endeavoured to create the 'communicator' to 'phone home' out of bits and pieces of everyday gadgets; what is of our interest here is the way how this old space man conceived of the construction of the communicator, that is, his 'mind-style' underlying his idea of the make-shift parabolic reflector.

In the last paragraph of the above citation, it goes: "... those early hints flashed at him from within, of a little fork dancing around a plate". In E.T.'s world (or universe!), it may be quite likely that an inanimate object like a fork may dance around a plate, as if it is an animate agent. This 'animation' of inanimate objects lead this old alien scientist to a series of procedures described earlier as in: "Torch-fingering his butter knife, he took out the temper, then bent and bolted it to the coat hanger, along with the fork, to form a ratchet device: knife and fork moved in and out of the teeth of the saw blade, advancing it tooth by tooth". It seems as if the knife and the fork are functioning as metaphorical agents which produce supersonic signals.

Incidentally, this seems to be quite the opposite of the imaginary world of Lok the Neanderthal, where even a human archer may not be perceived as a proper agent. However, needless to say, there is no scientific evidence again to prove that a creature like E.T. who is more intellectually superior to us is able to sense the agency of inanimate objects!

Setting aside the scientific fact again, it is clear from the above illustrations that one's cognition of agency differentiates one's mind-style or world-view a great deal. The other significant inspiration which can be drawn from the two episodes above is that the agency concept is very closely associated with that of 'animacy'. Both E.T. finding agency in a fork and Lok failing to do so in his modern enemy clearly represent different kinds of mind-style from the one we perceive as normal. This is because, in our more 'normal' mind-style, a *Homo sapiens* trying to snipe a Neanderthal can be a 'normal' agent, but a little fork which looks as if it is dancing around a plate cannot be a 'normal' agent. Why? In our 'normal' way of cognition, 'agency' is a faculty that is granted only to 'animate' beings but not to inanimate objects.

The agency concept presupposes that of animacy (cf. Klaiman 1991:113), and they both represent a fundamental aspect of linguistic structures which are highly significant determiners of mind-style or world-view (Fowler 1977:106). The close relationship which holds between agency and animacy will be explored in further detail in Section 2.5.

In bringing this section to a finish, yet another point regarding 'mind-style' must be made: from a point of view of literary stylistics, it must be noted that the concept of 'mind-style' can be more prototypically applied to the authors' epistemic attitudes, along with those of the characters as argued so far. Leech and Short construe the application of the term 'mind-style' to the analysis of one character (e.g. Lok) in one particular piece of work (e.g. William Golding's *The Inheritors*) as concerned with restricted domains of 'style'. "It is a commonplace that a writer's style reveals his habitual way of experiencing and interpreting things" (Leech & Short 1981:188). Consider the following sentence from John Steinbeck's *Of Mice and Men*:

(9) She screamed then, and Lennie's other hand closed over her mouth and nose.

In this scene, it is evident to the readers that Lennie is beginning to smother Curley's wife, but Steinbeck's way of putting it seems to relieve Lennie of much of the blame for his action. In the second clause, the incident is described as if Lennie's hand is the agent of the action of smothering the woman. Since Lennie is represented as a 'simpleton', Steinbeck regards it as appropriate that his agency, together with his intentionality and responsibility, should be diminished, and this reveals something about the author's value and a part of his mind-style or world-view (Leech & Short 1981:191).

Apart from the importance of the assignments of agency as a mirror of an author's mind-style, the above passage from *Of Mice and Men* carries yet another important implication. Articulation of agency highlights the responsibility of the agent; conversely, the suppression of agency in some measure results in reducing the responsibility of the (potential) agent. The major concern of the following section will be with how one's responsibility can be mitigated or maximised according to the mind-style of the authors who report the relevant event.

2.4 Political or ideological implications: Agency and responsibility

In the preceding section, it has been demonstrated how significantly the perception of human 'agency' affects our 'mind-style' and/or 'world-view', and as has been mentioned earlier, its pervasive effect can be consciously or unconsciously manipulated by particular use of language. Our major focus in the current section is upon this manipulation of the expression of agency, which typically lends itself to certain political manoeuvres particularly in the mass media.

As reported in a newspaper article in (10), in the mid-1980s, the locals in a Lancashire village were not very happy about driving along unreasonably stony roads, and the source of this problem was the lorries from a nearby quarry. Norman Fairclough, who is a local Lancastrian linguist himself, lucidly reveals the 'mind-style' of the author, through analysing his style of encoding the human agency and the accompanying responsibility which lurk behind the scene.

(10)   "Quarry load-shedding problem"
       Unsheeted lorries from Middlebarrow Quarry were still causing problems by shedding stones on their journey through Warton village, members of the parish council heard at their September meeting.
       The council's observations have been sent to the quarry management and members are hoping to see an improvement.

(*Lancaster Guardian*, 12 September 1986)

First of all, the title of this article, "Quarry load-shedding problem", is an example of 'nominalisation', a process expressed in the form of a noun phrase, as if it were an 'entity'. Fairclough argues that this grammatical form gives an effect of blurring the matter, unspecifying the agent in shedding loads or causing loads to be shed. We cannot tell, for the first instance, who or what is responsible for the 'problem' from this nominalised title (cf. Fairclough 1989: 51).

In the first paragraph of the main text of (10), the agency is attributed to 'unsheeted lorries from Middlebarrow Quarry'. The expression 'unsheeted' implies the failure of a process to happen – someone did not put sheets over the loads, when they ought to have done so. The *lorries* in this context serves as one form of metonymy, signifying a part of someone (or an inanimate instrument of someone) who are behind the scene and are actually responsible for the incident. Fairclough maintains that the 'hidden agents' are presumably 'the quarry management', who are, as found in the second paragraph, the recipients of the council's 'observations'. In other words, the inanimate lorries 'impersonalise' the hidden but real agents.

As in the above case, agency (and responsibility which naturally accompanies it) can be suppressed intentionally by means of particular grammatical styles, which have been selected from a myriad of stylistic possibilities. A further illustration can be provided through more detailed observation of the first part of the main text in (10), which actually consists of two clauses with the SVO structure type: *unsheeted lorries from Middlebarrow Quarry(S) were still causing(V) problems(O)* and *(lorries – 'understood' S) shedding(V) stones(O)*. Fairclough argues that the subject here is an untypical 'inanimate agent' of an action process which is typically represented by the SVO clausal pattern, and that agency in causing problems is attributed to the lorries, but not to the people who control them (1989: 123). As Davidson claims, attributions of agency are accusations or assignments of responsibility; it naturally follows then that non-attribution of agency means relief from responsibility. The use of a surface 'inanimate agent' to mitigate the sense of responsibility attributable to the 'real' agent is one form of the 'impersonalisation' of agency, which will be characterised in more detail in the following chapters.

In a different guise, it can also be argued that the use of SVO clauses with 'inanimate agents' as the subjects represents certain epistemic attitudes of authors of a particular kind, with their mind-style (or world-view) created through their particular ideological standpoint of relieving the powerful from their responsibility. However, Fairclough's terminology 'inanimate agent' needs to be handled with care; in Chapter 3, I will return to the thorough and consistent treatment of the exact concept which is labelled as such.

Fairclough's above example illustrates the typical 'mind-style' of the authors who write on behalf of the authorities, weakening or obfuscating their agency and thus mitigating their responsibility. The reverse also obtains. We can also search for cases where an article is written by an author with a reformist mind-style, who writes (or pretends to write) taking sides with the socially weak. Naturally, such writers tend to maximise the agency and hence the responsibility of those who are in power. The articles quoted in (11) and (12) below are taken from *Cambridge Town Crier* and *Cambridge Herald*, both of which address miscellaneous local problems in Cambridgeshire, where I am living at the time of writing this book. As a local resident, I hope I sound as convincing as Fairclough who talks about regional issues in his own county.

(11)   "Looking back on the News of 2003"

    a.   A campaign, supported by the *Town Crier*, is launched to save views at Grantchester Meadows. *Planners want to build up to 1,800 homes over-*

looking the beauty spot. In the midst of protests and petitions, *the county council delays a decision and asks the city council to study the site.*

b.   Plans for the proposed development overlooking Grantchester Meadows go on public display. The concerned residents' cause is later boosted *when ex-Pink Floyd star Roger Waters joins the campaign. Deputy Prime Minister John Prescott tells MP Andrew Lansley that he cannot have the plans stopped* because the decision is up to an "independent" panel of inspectors.

(*Cambridge Town Crier*, 2 January 2004)

(12)   "SAVED"
Proposals to build 1600 homes were described as likely to cause "irreparable environmental damage" in an independent report commissioned by the City Council.

The Herald supported a petition organised by Lib Dem Councillors against the plans. Over 3000 people signed the petition, some form [*sic*] as far away as Canada.

"This is an important victory," said David Howarth. "The Meadows are a vital green space for Cambridge – and are rightly famous across the world."

Cambridge's Labour MP, Anne Campbell, has supported the building plans.

(*The Cambridge Herald*, Winter 2003)

The two pieces of text above are concerned with the existing authority's 'evil' attempt to develop an enormous housing complex in a lovely green space called Grantchester Meadows, which is famous worldwide for its beauty and tranquillity (cf. Yamamoto 2003). Unlike Fairclough's example, the authors of the texts in (11) and (12) are not writing on behalf of the powerful but fiercely against the local authority's (and the central government's) plans. Their 'mind-style' of rebelling against the Labour Party government manifests itself in the form of intensified human agency found in the italicised clauses, which, except for one, have the SVO structure with human or semi-human entities as the subjects. I list them again for convenience in (13):

(13)   a.   Planners want to build up to 1,800 homes overlooking the beauty spot.
b.   ..., the county council delays a decision and asks the city council to study the site.
c.   ... ex-Pink Floyd star Roger Waters joins the campaign.
d.   Deputy Prime Minister John Prescott tells MP Andrew Lansley that he cannot have the plans stopped. ...
e.   *The Herald* supported a petition organised by Lib Dem Councillors against the plans.
f.   Over 3000 people signed the petition. ...
g.   "This is an important victory," said David Howarth.

h.   Cambridge's Labour MP, Anne Campbell, has supported the building plans.

In a series of struggles over the future of Grantchester Meadows, the involvement of intentional human agency is amplified in the two different senses: (1) the authors maximise the agency and intentionality of the existing local authority in an attempt to accuse their actions and pursue their responsibility, and (2) the writers also highlight the agency and the good intentions of their fellow activists to seek the publicity of their actions, since these articles are written for a certain ideological propaganda.

(13a), (13b), (13d) and (13h) are the examples which illustrate the cases of the first type, with intensified agency of the accused. The most typical examples of responsibility assignment are probably (13d) and (13h), where the use of a proper name singles out a particular individual as the target of the accusation. (13b) is an interesting example in the light of the animacy concept: the subject here *the county council* can be marked as a semi-human or semi-animate entity, since an organisation like this is not animate in itself, but a body of individual human beings, which acts on its own accounts. Accusation directed to an organisation seems to be somewhat blurred and indirect compared with that directed to particular individuals.

The rests, (13c), (13e), (13f) and (13g), belong to the second type, where the writers advertise their own campaigns. Again, referring to the agents by means of proper names seems to strengthen their agency the most, and thereby seek their publicity to the maximum, as can be observed in (13c) and (13g). What is interesting with the example (13f) is that the number of agents can naturally make their agency sound stronger, and this brings about the necessary effect to promote the writer's reformist propaganda.

The example (13e) contains a subject which is a human organisation, *The Herald*, and hence exhibits a similar phenomenon as seen in (13b); an agent lies on the borderline between animacy and inanimacy. The strength of animacy and that of agency seem to parallel each other and to be equally a matter of gradience of some measure; Section 2.5 will focus upon this relationship between animacy and agency, shedding light on how these potential cognitive scales can function in the use of our languages.

It seems a sensible idea to introduce here a general principle of human linguistic behaviours, which lurks behind the correlation between the encoding of agency (and the assignment of responsibility) and its resulting 'face threatening' effect. The articles which have been analysed so far are concerned with social problems but do not deal with any personal matters – so the writers naturally address the actions and events involving third person references rather than first and second person references. Brown and Levinson's (1978 and 1987) notion of 'FTAs', or face threatening acts, supplements our arguments above and explicates lucidly how first and second person referential expressions can encode strong agency and hence may threaten ones' 'faces'.

First and second person reference is inherently deictic, in that it makes direct reference to the speech act participants (Anderson & Keenan 1985:259; Halliday 1985:291; Lyons 1977:645), and it is this direct reference that encodes the perception of intentionality and responsibility strongly and thereby may carry face threatening effects. Brown and Levinson (1978:195–211) argue that English has several 'strategies' at its disposal to avoid explicit first and second person reference. The first of these is the use of verbs such as *appear*, *seem*, *look*, etc., as in:

(14) a. It appears/seems (to me) that ....
      b. It looks (to me) like ....

Instead of saying "I think that ....", the speaker can protect his/her own face by reducing (or not encoding at all) his/her agency with an impersonal dummy subject; 'impersonalisation' of 'self' is an effective means to save one's own face.

The speaker can benefit from the expressions such as above, escaping from a very strong agency and animacy which pertains to the first person singular personal pronoun and thus being psychologically released from the responsibility of what he/she says and its effect upon the addressee. Such responsibility is transmitted from 'I' to 'it' (Yamamoto 1999:75). Similarly, the speaker may prefer an expression like (15b) over (15a), so that the utterance will be less embarrassing to both the speaker and the addressee, with the shrunken sense of responsibility in making a rather unfortunate announcement.

(15) a. I regret that ....
      b. It is regretted that ....

Second person referential expressions can also be avoided, so as not to make direct reference to the addressee. When one wishes to reduce the burden and responsibility of the addressee and hence to make the chance of offending someone slimmer, he/she is more likely to say:

(16) If it is possible, ...

instead of saying:

(17) If you can, ...

with the direct reference to the addressee. Another strategy of the avoidance of explicit second person reference involves the use of the generic third person pronoun *one*, which is more likely to be found in writing.[11] These are also good examples of the 'impersonalisation' of agency, which can be made use of in order to mitigate the face threatening effect of what the speaker/writer intends to convey to the addressee.

As has been argued so far, our language enables us to manipulate the encoding of agency, responsibility and accusation by means of the selection of particular referential expressions and particular syntactic patterns. Through the course of our discussions, reference has been often made to the concept of animacy: for instance, by introducing inanimate subjects or an impersonal dummy pronoun 'it', one can obfuscate the human agency working behind the scene of the actions in question. The differentiation between the hierarchy of persons, i.e. the distinction between first, second and third persons, has also been mentioned, as well as the opposition between common nouns and proper nouns. All these issues will be addressed in a more systematised fashion in the following section.

2.5 Agency and 'animacy'

2.5.1 'Animacy' in general

Only animate beings can be agents in a normal sense. Fowler (1977:106) argues that the agency concept goes hand in hand with that of animacy, and that both notions are highly significant determiners of mind-style or world-view. As has been argued in Section 2.3, this inseparability between agency and animacy can explain very lucidly the stylistic characteristics of the protagonists' mind-styles in *The Inheritors* and *E.T.*

In our preceding arguments in Section 2.2, several ways of deconstructing the agency concept have been introduced, and one of them is the view proposed by Klaiman (1991:113) who argues that agency is premised on both animacy and awareness of action. I have already examined the latter half of her anatomy of agency, i.e. 'awareness of action', more or less leaving the first constituent animacy unexplained, although I mentioned such issues as (1) authors' strategic choice between animate and inanimate subjects, (2) the employment of 'semi-animate' entities as agents, (3) the difference between proper names and common nouns in terms of the assignment of agency and (4) the distinction between first, second and third person references. The distinction between proper names and common nouns and that between first, second and third persons may, at a glance, seem to be quite irrelevant to the notion of animacy, but their relevance to animacy will be made clear by the end of the present chapter.

'Animacy', which is an inseparable notion from that of agency, can be regarded as an assumed cognitive scale of some measure, extending from human through animate to inanimate. In addition to the 'life' concept itself, concepts related to that of life – such as locomotion, sentiency (including intentionality), etc. – can also be incorporated into the cognitive domain of 'animacy'. A common reflection of 'animacy' in a language is a distinction between animate and inanimate, and analogically, between human and non-human in one way or another (Yamamoto 1999: 1).

Such an overview of the animacy concept must naturally remind the readers of Aristotle's hierarchical account of the natural world; it is obvious that the word 'animacy' itself stems from the word *anima*, as in the title of Aristotle's work *De Anima*. As has been also mentioned in Section 2.2, Aristotle's central psychological notion of *psuchê*, possessed by all living things, is to be translated as 'animator' (Barnes 2000: 105), something that 'animates' or gives life to a living thing. In *De Anima*, Aristotle argues that different creatures are endowed with *psuchai*, or animators of different complexity, as illustrated in quotation (3) above, and that, on the basis of his taxonomy of nature, certain creatures – the so-called higher animals – are naturally marked out in virtue of enjoying consciousness and intentionality (Everson 1995: 168). His hierarchical view of 'animator' clearly corresponds to his classification of actions (as shown in the citation (2)), which are typically performed by living creatures of particular ranks.

As Comrie (1989: Ch. 9) argues, animacy is not a simple linear scale on which all individual entities that populate the world can be neatly arranged, but it reflects a natural human interaction amongst 'several different parameters' (Yamamoto 1999: Chs. 3–5). In establishing the conceptual framework of animacy, Yamamoto (1999) first of all dissects this notion into two parts: (1) animacy *per se* (or animacy in a literal sense) and (2) inferred animacy. Animacy *per se* is basically concerned with the central 'life' concept, i.e. a matter of the distinctive semantic feature [± alive], and encapsulates the natural hierarchical taxonomy of living creatures in terms of the generally held evolutionalist view and their fundamental physical faculties, such as locomotion.

The life concept is always intertwined with the possession of mind, as Aristotle's account of *psuchê* clearly illustrates. In exploring the relationship between children's social and non-social cognition, the psychologists Gelman and Spelke (1981: 49) state: "perhaps the most interesting aspect of the animate-inanimate distinction is the fact that only animate objects have minds". 'Inferred animacy' is a more psychological facet of the animacy concept, the origin of the term stemming from what is called 'inferred animism' in the field of infant psychology (Yamamoto 1999: 17). The psychologist Piaget (1926/1955: 190) reported an anecdote of a child who observed a marble rolling down a hill toward an adult companion and asked, "It knows that you are down there?". He argued that children view events in nature as "the reflection of a mental activity whose reasons or intentions the child is always trying to find out". Piaget called this type of phenomenon 'animistic' thinking, defining the term 'animism' as "the tendency to regard objects as living and endowed with will" (1929/1969: 170).

However, Tunmer argues that Piaget's above definition of 'animism' is insuf-
ficient, because one of the consequences of this definition is that the 'life' concept
and concepts related to it (such as 'intentionality') are interdependent. Alterna-
tively, Tunmer draws a line between the life concept proper, which is a matter of
the semantic feature [± alive], and its derivative concepts, dissecting childhood
animism into two aspects: (1) animism *per se* (attributing 'life' itself to inanimate
objects) and (2) 'inferred' animism (endowing inanimate objects with sentiency)
(Tunmer 1985: 990). By the same rationale, it seems reasonable to assume that the
concept of animacy also consists of two different aspects: animacy *per se* (or animacy in its literal sense) and 'inferred' animacy, mostly mental aspects of animacy
deriving from the life concept proper, including sentiency and the attribution of
empathy, etc.

In explicating the notion of animacy as a complex of animacy *per se* and inferred animacy, it seems sensible to explore it in terms of several closely related
parameters, the boundaries between each one of them being rather hazy. As I have
previously proposed (Yamamoto 1999), the kernel of the notion of animacy is (A)
the General Animacy Scale, which is an assumed cognitive scale, concerning the
ontological status of the animate and inanimate entities that populate this world.
In terms of our cognitive and linguistic realisation of the animacy concept, this
main scale interacts with other parameters: (B) the Hierarchy of Persons, (C) the
Individuation Scale and, finally, (D) the Participant (Semantic) Role Scale or the
Agency Scale (cf. Yamamoto 1999: 2).[12]

First and foremost, the General Animacy Scale is *based* on a kind of hierarchy
of animacy *per se* with the assumed natural taxonomy regarding the hierarchy of
living things, which extends from human through animal to inanimate, if defined
with certain oversimplification. However, it is in fact important to realise that certain aspects of inferred animacy are very difficult to sever from animacy *per se*.
This is why Aristotle argues that all animate beings enjoy the faculty of *psuchai*
of different complexity, depending on their stature; he could not help taking into
account the mental characteristics of living beings when he classifies them in the
right order, with higher animals endowed with consciousness and intentionality.[13]
This means that the General Animacy Scale is actually an amalgam of animacy
in its literal sense and such factors as sentiency which constitutes a major part of
inferred animacy.

It is also important to bear in mind that this hierarchical classification of animate beings and inanimate objects is the product of our subjective view of these
entities; hence the General Animacy Scale is subject to our more fine-grained cognitive processes, which, for instance, make us feel that cats are more 'animate'
than scallops, and that organisations, such as '*The Cambridge Herald*' and 'the
city council', behave (or appear to behave) as if they are animate beings which
have a will of their own, despite their obvious inanimacy. One may also say that

those who find more sentiency in cats than in monkeys possess one possible id-iosyncratic variant of the General Animacy Scale, in which cats are placed higher than monkeys.

Unavoidably, we can observe the outside world from our own egocentric per-spective as humans. The cognitive scale of animacy seems to operate in such an anthropocentric way that the human category is given a specially superior sta-tus to those of any other animate entities, although, scientifically speaking, *Homo sapiens* are no more 'animate' than even amoebae! (Again, those who find more sentiency and intelligence in cats than in humans may not share the same picture of 'animacy hierarchy' with most other fellow humans.)

As Myhill (1992: 38) points out, linguists often dispense with a clear-cut differ-entiation between the opposition of animate/inanimate and that of human/non-human, and this is not to be regarded as merely imprecise. Linguists sometimes mix up the notion of animacy with that of 'humanness' or 'personhood', presup-posing, perhaps unconsciously, that humans are the supreme representatives of all animate beings, and there seem to be two major reasons for this (Yamamoto 1999: 9–10). Firstly, linguists (and all of us) are human beings and investigate human language from their own anthropocentric points of view. Secondly, it is generally the case that human languages, since they are made use of by humans, talk far more often about humans than about any other creatures on the earth (or on the other planets); so much so that the manifestations of the boundary be-tween these two categories tend to be rather hazy. The concept of 'humanness' or 'personhood', as well as the 'self' concept, has been assumed to be a cultural univer-sal (Hallowell 1958). Miller and Johnson-Laird (1976: 102) further argue that the concept 'person' is a psychological primitive, unanalysable concept. This inevitable intervention of 'personhood' in our conceptualisation of animacy will have to be borne in mind, when characterising the other interacting parameters, particularly, (B) the Hierarchy of Persons.

In observing the actual manifestations of animacy in our use of language, it seems necessary to consider some borderline cases, particularly those involving metaphor or metonymy of some sort. There are several relatively clear (but in a subjective sense) borderline cases between animacy and inanimacy on the General Animacy Scale: particular kinds of modern machines which operate in a rather human way, (human) organisations and geographical entities or local communi-ties are perhaps the most eminent examples. For instance, one may often attribute certain 'intelligence' or 'cleverness' to computers, which can perform very compli-cated mathematical tasks and hence look far more intellectually superior to human beings, fostering our metaphorical sense of animacy/agency (Yamamoto 1999: 18). Computers sometimes look even intentional; we can easily imagine someone curs-ing his/her computer when it 'misbehaved' most probably because of mechanical faults or 'bugs' (but not because of its bad intention), yelling as in:

(18)   I'll hit you, if you do that again!

Note that *you* in (18) refers to the speaker's computer. The cognitive significance of using the second person personal pronoun here will be made clearer below, when we consider the basic characteristics of the Hierarchy of Persons.

The ontological status of organisations and geographical entities/local communities seems to be far more subtle than that of human-like machines, which are physically inanimate. Human organisations (and geographical entities/local communities) are not physically alive themselves and, accordingly, are not animate in terms of animacy *per se*, but it is these entities which can be regarded as the real borderline cases between animacy and inanimacy (Yamamoto 1999:18), in that they consist of a body of individual human beings, as well as of their buildings and other facilities. They make their own decisions, as if they were individual human beings. Sometimes, individual human beings may speak for an organisation or a local community to which they belong, as if they were the institution themselves. Two examples we considered in the previous section illustrate the rather animate-like – and rather agent-like – nature of human organisations:

(19)   a.   ..., the county council delays a decision and asks the city council to study the site.   (*Cambridge Town Crier*, 2 January 2004)
       b.   *The Herald* supported a petition organised by Lib Dem Councillors against the plans.   (*The Cambridge Herald*, Winter 2003)

Examples of animate-like use of geographical entities and local communities are provided in (20) below:

(20)   a.   BMW's £800m take over means that, for the first time in 112 years, Britain no longer boasts a British-owned volume car maker.
                                                                (*The Independent*, 1 February 1994)
       b.   Furious Moscow condemns 'ridiculous' Western action and demands Security Council meeting.   (*The Times*, 12 April 1994)
       c.   *Ōsaka wa kono ken   niwa   hantai   rashii.*
            Ōsaka TOP this   issue   about   against   seem.
            'Osaka seems to be against us concerning this issue'.
                                                                (Yamamoto 1999:21)

In the English examples of (20a) and (20b) and the Japanese example of (20c), *Britain*, *Moscow* and *Ōsaka* are the names of places or, by metonymic extension, communities whose members 'no longer boast a British-owned volume car maker', 'condemn "ridiculous" Western action' or 'seem to be against us concerning this issue'. A general principle of metonymy, by which a place may stand for a group of human beings residing in the place, is at work in these examples (Lakoff & Johnson 1980:Ch. 8), where geographical entities are referred to as if they are sentient beings and hence attributed a touch of (rather weak) metaphorical agency.

An example of metonymic use of an 'inanimate agent' is discussed in Section 2.4 after Fairclough (1989):

(21)   Unsheeted lorries from Middlebarrow Quarry were still causing problems by shedding stones on their journey through Warton village, ...

(*Lancaster Guardian*, 12 September 1986)

As argued earlier, the expression *unsheeted lorries from Middlebarrow Quarry* in (21) is a good example of metonymy, which signifies a part of someone who is behind the scene. Unlike the entities found in (19) and (20), the unsheeted lorries here look quite inanimate, although it is still possible to argue that they are imbued with a weak touch of metaphorical inferred animacy (and agency). A 'lorry' is a less typical instance of the borderline case between animacy and inanimacy, although it is quite a human-like modern machine with headlights as eyes and carries its driver, who is a human being.

However, even highly inanimate of entities – including what we may not even call an 'entity' – can be endowed with animate-like and agent-like onto-logical status by the force of figurative use of language. Let us examine again the above-mentioned quotation from *E.T.* as repeated in (22) below:

(22)   Torch-fingering his butter knife, he took out the temper, then bent and bolted it to the coat hanger, along with the fork, to form a ratchet device: knife and fork moved in and out of the teeth of the saw blade, advancing it tooth by tooth.

Here, in the world of science fiction, the 'animation' of knife and fork by the spell of the little old alien makes them function as if these inanimate objects are 'metaphorical agents'.

To a certain extent, it seems necessary to accept the notion of 'metaphorical animacy' and 'metaphorical agency', which are expressed by the figurative use of language. After all, it is language users (not only speakers and writers but also hear-ers and addresses in some cases) who subjectively 'breathe' animacy (and agency which is premised on it) of different strength into various referring expressions and the entities that surround us themselves (cf. Yamamoto 1999:23). We will come back to the problem of figurative speech in Chapter 5, with more exam-ples of poetic expressions in both English and Japanese and with reference to the rhetorical notion of 'pathetic fallacy'.

2.5.2 The interacting parameters

The 'secondary' parameters which interact with the core (A) General Animacy Scale – i.e. (B) the Hierarchy of Persons, (C) the Individuation Scale and (D) the Agency Scale (or the Participant/Semantic Role Scale) - are all concerned with specific aspects of inferred animacy, but the motivation for introducing them is to make use of them for the analysis of animacy reflected in various facets of human language.

The Hierarchy of 'Persons' is concerned mostly with the human category which is distinguished from other animate and inanimate categories by the General Animacy Scale. As I have argued above, the 'personhood' concept unavoidably interferes with the characterisation of animacy, because (1) we humans investigate our language from our anthropocentric view of the world and (2) human beings generally talk more about human beings than about other animate beings. The concept 'personhood' can also be regarded as a 'cultural universal' (Hallowell 1958) and a 'psychological primitive' (Miller & Johnson-Laird 1976).

Basically, the Hierarchy of Persons can be described as a 'linguistic device', which is particularly useful when we consider the linguistic manifestations of animacy and agency through observing a variety of referential expressions, as demonstrated in our preceding discussion on face threatening acts (see Section 2.4). From an anthropocentric point of view, it can be argued that a basic distinction is to be made between first person (primarily speaker(s)), second person (primarily addressee(s)) and third person (others) within the human category. (Theoretically speaking, however, there can be a case where the speaker is a water flea, who is talking to an amoeba about some remarkable ascidians living in the sea!) Many scholars have argued that first and second persons are higher in animacy than third person (cf. for instance, Silverstein 1976; Foley & Van Valin 1985; Croft 1990 & 2003; Dixon 1994; Langacker 1991; Palmer 1994; Yamamoto 1999).

This is partly because of the notion of 'empathy' which is closely associated with animacy. It is natural that the speaker invests the strongest animacy and empathy in himself/herself, and the second strongest animacy/empathy in someone whom he/she is talking to (cf. Langacker 1991). It is also important to point out that first and second persons are intrinsically deictic; this deictic nature entails direct reference to the speech act participants, attributing stronger senses of animacy, agency and responsibility to the referents than in the cases of indirect reference.

The third cognitive scale characterising the animacy concept is (C) the Individuation Scale. In a nutshell, the term 'individuation' means the degree to which we perceive something as a 'clearly delimited and identifiable entity' (Dahl & Fraurud 1993). The Individuation Scale is particularly useful when it comes to the linguistic explanation in terms of animacy of the contrast between singular and plural forms and the use of different types of noun phrases, such as personal pronouns,[14] proper names and common noun phrases. Associated psychologically with the opposition between immediacy and remoteness (or directness and indirectness), the singularity/plurality distinction can affect the degree of animacy which is encoded by a referential expression in question.

Plurality often weakens the sense of animacy and agency/responsibility, impersonalising and obfuscating the identity of the referent. For instance, from the sentence *We regret that* ... in a letter conveying a bad news, it can be naturally inferred that the persons responsible for the rather unfortunate announcement are an ambiguous, impersonal body consisting of at least more than two people, whereas when the expression *I regret that* ... is used instead, the one who is responsible is the writer himself/herself, who exercises strong agency over the matter. One example of an exception to this can be the case where 'over 3000 people' manifest stronger animacy and agency than a single individual, which has been discussed in the previous section:

(23)   Over 3000 people signed the petition, some form [*sic*] as far away as Canada.
                                                    (*The Cambridge Herald*, Winter 2003)

Similarly, there is also a significant difference between addressing or referring to someone by their name (such as 'David' or 'John Prescott') and doing so by their role (such as 'the Lib Dem Councillor' or 'Deputy Prime Minister'). The addressees or the referents are treated more as individual humans in the former cases than in the latter, where it can be interpreted that they are regarded as 'institutionalised' and 'impersonal' representatives of roles and functions. It naturally follows then that, as argued in the previous section, the referents' inferred animacy and agency can be highlighted by using a proper name as in (24a), whereas, as in (24b), they can be significantly weakened if the same individual is referred to only by means of a common noun which only designates his/her role or function in the society:

(24)   a.   Cambridge's Labour MP, Anne Campbell, has supported the building
            plans.   (*The Cambridge Herald*, Winter 2003)
        b.   The Labour MP in Cambridge has supported the building plans.

Finally, here comes (D) the Agency Scale or the Participant (Semantic) Role Scale. It should be noted, however, that this parameter possesses a fundamentally different status from those of the other scales discussed so far. Whilst (A) the General Animacy Scale, (B) the Hierarchy of Persons and (C) the Individuation Scale are concerned with the ontological properties of miscellaneous animate and inanimate entities themselves that populate the world, this parameter, (D) the Agency Scale, is a matter of the particular kinds of relationship into which such animate and inanimate entities enter through their 'actions' or the events and processes they are engaged in.

Animacy is a matter of gradience, and so is agency. The general (and somewhat oversimplified) principle is: the stronger the animacy of a certain entity is in terms of (A) the General Animacy Scale, (B) the Hierarchy of Persons and (C) the Individuation Scale, the stronger its agency can be. However, the agency concept inevitably incorporates the 'verbal' aspects of the events or actions that we report in a clause. In fact, in the use of our language, the strength of agency carried by certain expressions referring to various animate beings can be determined partly by their ontological status concerning animacy and sentiency (including intentionality and consciousness/awareness), and partly by the nature of actions in which such entities are involved, such actions being expressed by verb phrases.

In this section, agency has been regarded as one of the conceptual properties of animacy, but as we have observed through the arguments by Fowler (1977) and Klaiman (1991), the reverse also obtains: the agency concept presupposes that of animacy. They are the main constituent of each other, both sharing a hierarchical nature which is a fundamental cognitive measure of our understanding of the world. In fact, the notion of agency captures the most animate-like aspects of animate beings (Yamamoto 1999: 147).

Aristotle granted only higher animals, who/which are therefore highly animate, the faculty of intentionality and consciousness, which naturally embraces 'awareness of action'. This means that amongst the conceptual constituents of agency, animacy is the most fundamental; for instance, 'intentionality' forms a part of 'sentiency', which forms a part of 'inferred animacy'. 'Inferred animacy', together with 'animacy *per se*', constructs the entire picture of the animacy concept. Accordingly, there will be constant recourse to this correlation between animacy and agency throughout the linguistic discussions which will be unfolded in the forthcoming chapters.

CHAPTER 3

Linguistic treatment of agency and its manifestations in Japanese and English

With reference to the concept of 'impersonality'

MIA
He fell out of a window.
VINCENT
That's one way to say it. Another way is, he was thrown out. Another way is, he was thrown out by Marsellus. And even another way is, he was thrown out of a window by Marsellus because of you. (Quentin Tarantino, *Pulp Fiction*)

3.1 Overview

As has been argued in Chapter 2, the 'agency' concept can be 'deconstructed' in a couple of ways, and it presupposes the notions of 'intentionality' and 'animacy', which have traditionally been associated with it. It was also argued that agency is inseparable from such factors as 'awareness of action' and 'responsibility'. The degree to which we encode human agency in our language can sometimes be manipulated by means of particular grammatical forms and particular types of referential expressions – either consciously or unconsciously.

The above quotation from Quentin Tarantino's *Pulp Fiction* provides a good example here. Mia and Vincent are talking about a big, fat man, who used to be Vincent's 'colleague' and was dubbed 'Tony Rocky Horror'. Mia's husband, Marsellus, who is the boss of both men, sent a couple of blokes to this 'Tony Rocky Horror', and they took him out on his patio and threw him over the balcony. The big, fat man fell four stories and, since then, he developed a speech impediment.

Mia, who is suspected to be the source of this tragedy, does not seem to understand the situation well and expresses the event as: "He fell out of a window". Vincent, on the other had, has been quite horrified with the idea of his mate being nearly killed by his boss and tries to seek someone's agency behind the whole situation, but, since Mia is his boss' wife, he cannot express his idea too directly; as a result, he expresses the event in question in a passive sentence: "And even another way is, he was thrown out of a window by Marsellus because of you". Vincent had been asked by Marsellus to escort his wife on the evening when the big boss was away and was naturally in fear of the same kind of tragedy happening to him this time.

In this chapter, the foci of our attention will be upon the actual linguistic manifestations of agency, which illustrate the distinct 'mind-styles' of language users; specifically, the styles of encoding agency in the Japanese and English languages will be contrastively analysed on the basis of statistical data, revealing the distinct mind-styles of their speakers. In Chapter 1, the point has already been made that whereas Japanese tends to 'cover up' agency in constructing a clause, English, as its default value, tends to articulate human agency in expressing a certain proposition, although, of course, there are plenty of cases where the English speakers/writers obfuscate agency as observed in the case of the "Quarry load-shedding problem" in *Lancaster Guardian*. But, in general, Japanese is a language which prefers to describe an event as Mia did, whilst English is more like Vincent who tries to clarify who did what.

Before embarking upon the analyses of concrete linguistic data, some notable remarks on the treatment of agency in linguistics must be reviewed to provide a certain theoretical framework. Section 3.2 will describe how linguists chased the enigmatic notion of agency into the corner of a tiny box, in an attempt to pin it down within the restriction of grammatical theories. The grammatical device which will be at our disposal is the characterisation of semantic roles by the Functional Grammar developed by Dik (1989), Siewierska (1991 and 1993), etc., despite some obvious theoretical defects. As it will be made clear later, their treatment of agency seems to go hand in hand with the philosophical (or conceptual) characterisation of the agency concept presented in Chapter 2.

In Section 3.3, the contrastive ways of encoding agency will be observed through a number of examples from the Japanese and the English languages. The classical assumption concerning the opposition between the primacy of 'action' and that of 'event' will first be illustrated and later verified through examining Ikegami's (1982 and 1991) 'hypotheses'. Most of the examples that we will consider have been extracted from the relatively small-sized parallel corpora consisting of the two languages (whose structure and basic merits will be explicated later), and, on the basis of solid statistical arguments resulting from case studies on the corpora, the conspicuous tendencies of suppressing *vs.* expressing agency which Japanese and English exhibit respectively, will be brought into broad daylight.

We will also consider the possible reasons behind the result of corpus analysis. Section 3.3 will have recourse to the contrast between 'impersonal' *vs.* highly 'agentive' construction of clauses, that are prevalent in Japanese and English respectively, in an attempt to illustrate the typical epistemic attitude underlying the treatment of agency in the two languages. A particular focus will be upon the concept of 'impersonality' or 'impersonalness', when discussing the notable features of

Japanese person reference. 'Impersonality', which appears in the title of this book and is one of our major concerns in Chapters 3 and 4, designates an impersonal nuance brought about by the 'anti-agentive' ways of expressing actions and events that are typical of the Japanese language.

3.2 Agency in linguistic analysis

3.2.1 Inanimate agents and 'verbal' aspect of agency

In the last chapter, I argued that 'animacy' is a notion which is traditionally associated with that of agency and is one of the indispensable 'ingredients' in the characterisation of agency. However, at the same time, it is necessary to keep the fact in sight that agency and animacy are different, independent concepts, however closely they are correlated with each other. The distinction between them is actually quite clear: whereas 'animacy' is concerned with the intrinsic features and ontological status of animate and inanimate entities themselves, the notion of 'agency' characterises the entities (at least partially) according to what they are 'doing' (Yamamoto 1999: 149–150).

Agency is, in a way, a matter of relations which a particular entity enters into when it becomes involved in a certain 'action' (cf. Section 2.5). When it comes to the linguistic realisation of animacy and agency, in a nutshell, the former is largely a matter of noun phrases, whereas the latter is concerned with verb phrases; however, as has been observed in the preceding chapters, it must be borne in mind that agency is also a matter of the various inherent natures of agents themselves. This subsection will explore how 'agency' has been incorporated into 'purely linguistic' discussions, beginning with the argument regarding the relationship between the lexical meaning of verb phrases and the attribution of agency by Cruse (1973), who focussed almost exclusively on the verbal aspect of the agency concept.

Cruse argues that the agency concept should be characterised in terms of the feature of the meaning of the surface lexical item *do* (1973: 11). He maintains that this approach is a 'purely linguistic' one, as opposed to a 'referential' approach, which is concerned not only with the features of a verb phrase, but also with the inherent characteristics of a noun phrase, that signifies the agent itself. The referential position can be clearly observed in Fillmore's well-quoted definition of the 'agentive case':

(1)   ... the case of the typically animate perceived instigator of the action identified by the verb
                                                                    (Fillmore 1968: 24)

Fillmore's definition of the 'agentive case' is quite congruous with Klaiman's (1991) view of the agency concept, which has been examined in Chapter 2, in that they both assume that agency presupposes animacy, although Fillmore's expression 'animate perceived instigator' may allow some metaphorically animate entities to be possible agents. One potential problem with Fillmore's argument here lies in the word 'instigator': as stated in Section 2.2, many modern philosophers, including Davidson and Thalberg, aired scepticism on the necessity of including the notion of 'causation' or 'causality' as a constituent of agency. However, as far as the relationship between causation/causality and agency is concerned, we shall not go any further to avoid being drugged into the complex philosophical muddle of centuries and to keep everything else bouncing along.

Cruse's (1973:11) major criticism on Fillmore's 'referential' definition of agency is that if the agentive case is to be defined in this way, there would be "no way of identifying inanimate agents". In comparing the sentences *John overturned the dustbin* and *The wind overturned the dustbin*, Cruse argues, it is difficult to see how *the wind* is any less an agent than *John*, and what makes both *the wind* and *John* equally agentive is the nature of what they *do*, i.e. overturning the dustbin. He supports this point by referring to the sun, wind, frost, etc. which are commonly called 'natural agents' without being attributed animacy (Cruse 1973:11). Thus, he draws the conclusion that it is pointless to take into account whether a performer of an action is animate, and that the characterisation of agency should be made only on the ground of the nature of the activity (or the relation into which a particular animate or inanimate entity enters), which is most clearly manifested in the lexical meaning of verb phrases.

As the philosophers such as Davidson and Thalberg have pointed out, one of the popular means of pinning down the agency concept is to establish its 'grammatical litmus'. Cruse proposes one which he dubs the 'do-test'. The do-test is designed to distinguish 'actions' from 'non-actions', selecting verbs which are hyponymous to *do*:

(2)   ... or, more exactly (since in some cases the nature of the subject determines whether or not the verb is hyponymous to *do*), it [the do-test] selects sentences *NP VP* such that *NP VP* is hyponymous to *NP (do) something*. The assumption is made that *NP (do) something* manifests the feature of agentivity in a more or less pure form.   (Cruse 1973:14)

The examples in (3) and (4) illustrate one way in which this diagnostic formula can be actually implemented, using the logical concept of necessary implication or entailment.

(3)   *John broke the vase* entails *John did something*.

(4)   *The vase broke* does not entail *The vase did something*.

In (3), *John*, who broke the vase, passes the do-test since he *did something*, but *the vase* in (4) does not pass the test since it did not *do* anything, but just broke.

Although Cruse admits that "in some cases the nature of the subject determines whether or not the verb is hyponymous to *do*", he argues that inanimate entities can be perfect agents by virtue of their kinetic or other energy, and that the verb *do* can be used in the following way (Cruse 1973:16–17):

(5)   a.   What the wind *did* was blow the tree down.
      b.   What the computer is *doing* is calculating the correlation coefficient.
      c.   What the bullet *did* was smash John's collar-bone.

The sentences in (5a) to (5c) are grammatically correct. However, from a 'referential' point of view, it must be noted here that they all contain a more or less figurative use of language, i.e. personification, which gives the inanimate entities a touch of metaphorical 'inferred animacy' (Yamamoto 1999:14–24). Conversely, the verbal aspects of the sentences in (5a), (5b) and (5c) describe what are considered completely normal and realistic, and the 'kinetic or other energy' does not add anything special: the wind is no longer the wind when it does not blow, and a bullet is of no use if it is incapable of smashing someone's collar-bone!

It would be a little more difficult to reach a similar decision with (6a) below (Palmer 1981:149), whose subject also passes Cruse's do-test as in (6b):

(6)   a.   The virus killed the organism.
      b.   What the virus *did* was kill the organism.

The obvious difficulty in judging whether *the virus* is an agent or not lies in the question of whether 'virus' is animate; it is one of the most prototypical 'borderline cases' between animacy and inanimacy that we argued in Section 2.5. As Palmer (1981:149) points out, another difficult problem is with *my ear* in (7a), which is certainly 'doing something' as demonstrated in (7b):

(7)   a.   My ear is twitching.
      b.   What my ear is *doing* is twitching.

It is difficult to rule out the possibility of characterising 'my ear' as animate, as far as 'I' am alive, but whether or not we should grant the faculty of independent intentionality to one's ear (or other body parts) is yet another problematic question (cf. our former discussion concerning Lok's view on agency), the answer to which may be different from individual to individual.

Moreover, some examples of 'inanimate agents' further undermine Cruse's point that agency should be defined only in terms of the surface lexical meaning of verb phrases. Consider again the following example from the article "Quarry load-shedding problem" in *Lancaster Guardian*:

(8)   *Unsheeted lorries from Middlebarrow Quarry* were still causing problems by shedding stones on their journey through Warton village, ….

(*Lancaster Guardian*, 12 September 1986)

As argued in the preceding chapter, the 'unsheeted lorries from Middlebarrow Quarry' are clearly examples of what can be termed as 'inanimate agents' (Fairclough 1989). Agency is metaphorically attributed to the inanimate lorries in order to obfuscate the responsibility of the 'hidden (real) agents' whose 'metonymic part' is the unsheeted lorries shedding stones on the roads in a Lancashire village, and these lorries can also pass the do-test *a la* Cruse, as in:

(9)   What the unsheeted lorries from Middlebarrow Quarry *did* was shed stones on their journey through Warton village.

According to Fairclough (1989:51), this article was written by someone who wishes to suppress the agency, intentionality and responsibility of the people in authority; if the 'unsheeted lorries from Middlebarrow Quarry' is no less agentive than, say, 'the managing director of the quarry', simply because the lorries *did something*, there would be no point at all to manipulate the strength of agency by means of an 'inanimate agent' in the first place (cf. our previous discussions in Section 2.4).

The incapability of the 'do-test' of explaining the stylistic manipulation involving inanimate agents lies in Cruse's overestimation of the surface lexical meaning of verb phrases in defining agency. As Hundt (2004:49) argues, the notion of agency is characterised in the context of constructing a whole sentence, which involves both nominal and verbal constituents, and "features [of agency] are assigned to a noun phrase relative to the event that is referred to by the predicate" (Schlesinger 1995:40).

Of course, the agency concept itself presupposes that of 'action', but at the same time, it encapsulates a complex of other elements such as animacy, intentionality, responsibility and awareness of action, which are largely attributable to the inherent, ontological status of agents, as argued by Aristotle for example. Accordingly, the framework to be employed in the further study of the linguistic manifestations of agency must be capable of capturing not only the 'purely linguistic' aspect of agency, but its 'referential' aspect with various pragmatic implications stemming from the nature of the potentially agentive entities involved. The following subsection is an endeavour in search for the most suitable linguistic framework for our current project.

3.2.2 Grammatical machinery

In terms of its surface grammatical manifestation, agency is a matter of both noun phrases, which are concerned with the ontological nature of agents themselves, and verb phrases, illustrating the activities in which potential agents are involved, and, therefore, has been captured in a number of different ways in the linguistic tradition of the recent past. Just citing a few, Gruber (1967: 943) speaks of 'agentive verbs', Fillmore (1968: 24) advocates an 'agentive case', and Lyons (1968: 364–366), Leech (1981: 31, 185, 209) and many others talk about 'agentive nouns'.

Amongst all, particularly influential is the notion of agency as a grammatical 'case' – or, in a different guise, a 'semantic role' – proposed by Charles Fillmore, the founder of (the main-stream) Case Grammar theory. On the ground of its conceptual importance, Fillmore treats agency (or agentivity) as the core of the relations which explain how a particular participant or entity is involved in the situation described by a predicate. He introduces a number of principal cases, which can be assigned to noun phrases in a sentence and are widely applicable, including 'Agent', 'Patient', 'Instrumental', etc., as well as somewhat peripheral cases, such as 'Locative'.

Gruber (1967) and his successors, on the other hand, view things quite differently and propose that in the heart of state of affairs are general 'locative' cases, such as 'Goal' and 'Source'; therefore, their approach has often been labelled as 'localistic'.[1] Although 'Goal' and 'Source' are prototypically accompanied by verbs of motion, they can be metaphorically applied to more abstract propositions. According to the localistic version of semantic role assignment, an 'agent' in a Fillmorean sense, such as *Peter* in *Peter is reading the classical Japanese texts*, can be subsumed under the role of 'Source', as well as a literary source of motion like *Amsterdam* in *Kees departs from Amsterdam* and an experiencer of a physical sensation such as *Peter* in *Peter is freezing in front of his house*. This localistic approach does not articulate the primary status of agency in the taxonomy of semantic roles and, therefore, does not seem to be an appropriate model for our present purpose. Since the main interest of this book is in agency rather than in spatial (and temporal) elements, our foci will be upon Fillmore's 'agentive' interpretation of semantic roles and that of his followers. Fillmore's basic insights have been taken up by Chafe (1970) and other Case Grammarians, by the 'Functional Grammars' of Dik (1978 and 1989), Givón (1984) and Foley and Van Valin (1984), and by Dowty (1991), who proposed the interesting notions of 'Proto-Agent' and 'Proto-Patient' (for the process of this theoretical development, see Primus 1999: 49).

Amongst the variants of Case Grammars *a la* Fillmore, uniquely noteworthy is Chafe's (1970: 109) treatment of 'inanimate agents'; he proposes the concept of 'potent' to comprehend both animate and inanimate entities which are conceived of having their own motivating force. The potent concept covers not only the 'natural agents' (cf. Cruse 1973) but also such entities as *the ship* in *The ship destroyed the pier*, which cannot be identified as 'instrumental'. This treatment of inanimate force is reminiscent of the above-mentioned interpretation of agency by Cruse. What we need here is a convincing and consistent grammatical device, which is made use of to sensibly distinguish between prototypical, animate agents and 'inanimate agents'. Since the agency concept presupposes that of animacy, it seems reasonable to treat physically inanimate entities as non-agents, except when they are imbued with a very strong sense of inferred animacy and take on human-like forces and volitions in a metaphorical (and more or less 'fictional') piece of discourse. A Functional Grammarian, Simon Dik (1989), proposes two separate roles of 'Agent' and 'Force', the latter characterising inanimate entities capable of the power to cause the world to change.

Despite a few shortcomings which will be examined in the later part of this subsection, the theoretical framework of Functional Grammar developed by Dik (henceforth, abbreviated as 'FG') can be regarded as an appropriate model for our current discussion on the grammatical manifestation of agency, because the FG treatment of agency embraces both animacy and intentionality as the indispensable elements which define the characteristics of the role of 'Agent', thus perfectly conforming to our previous philosophical arguments.

The FG approach to agency (and semantic roles in general) is based on the typology of 'state of affairs' (often abbreviated as 'SoA'), which is the differentiation of situations and events that a particular predicate may designate (Siewierska 1991:43). Such states of affairs are classified into six categories in terms of the three key concepts: 'dynamicity', 'control' and 'telicity', as in the matrix shown in (10), which illustrates the types of state of affairs distinguished in FG and how they are determined through these key notions (Dik 1989:98):

(10) | SoA type | [dynamicity] | [control] | [telicity] |
|---|---|---|---|
| * Situation | − | | |
| * * Position | − | + | |
| * * State | − | − | |
| * Event | + | | |
| * * Action | + | + | |
| * * * Accomplishment | + | + | + |
| * * * Activity | + | + | − |
| * * Process | + | − | |
| * * * Change | + | − | + |
| * * * Dynamism | + | − | − |

Amongst the three key notions in the FG classification of state of affairs, 'dynamicity' is the most fundamental concept which first of all puts all state of affairs in two categories: 'Situations' and 'Events'. Then both 'Situations' and 'Events' are to be subcategorised according to the feature of 'control', which has been closely associated with agency; 'Situations' can be divided into 'Positions' and 'States', and 'Events' into 'Actions' and 'Processes'. Finally, the telicity notion further distributes the subcategories of 'Events', i.e. 'Actions' and 'Processes', into more fine-grained orders: 'Accomplishments', 'Activities', 'Changes' and 'Dynamisms'. Here are some examples of the six subcategories of SoA types distinguished in (10) (Dik 1989:97):

(11)   a.   John kept his money in an old sock. (Position)
       b.   John's money is in an old sock. (State)
       c.   John ran the marathon in three hours. (Accomplishment)
       d.   John was reading a book. (Activity)
       e.   The apple fell from the tree. (Change)
       f.   The clock was ticking. (Dynamism)

How can 'agency' be captured in this functionalist framework? To obtain a clearer idea of the importance of agency in Functional Grammar, it seems necessary to explore how the three features of dynamicity, control and telicity interact with agency. In a nutshell, the agency concept can be analysed in terms of the first two parameters, i.e. dynamicity and control, but the feature of telicity, which is concerned only with whether a certain event or situation is completed or not, is not of direct relevance to the determination of agency.

First of all, according to our basic intuition, an 'action' must be 'dynamic' in one way or another; given this fundamental characteristic of the notion of 'action', it is natural that 'dynamicity' is of significant relevance to agency amongst the three key parameters of FG. More specifically, agency can be regarded as relevant only to the state of affairs which is [+ dynamic], i.e. 'Event' in Dik's terminology. It should be noted here that 'action' has traditionally been classified as one of the subcategories of 'event' in the rigorous philosophical characterisation of agency, as envisaged in Chapter 2. This philosophical insight seems to be congruous with the FG classification of state of affairs as exhibited in (10).

Basically, 'dynamicity' in an FG sense can be explicated in relation to the notion of 'change'; non-dynamic states of affairs do not involve any change and remain constant, whereas dynamic states of affairs comprehend changes of a certain measure (Siewierska 1991:53). The notion of 'change', on which the dynamicity parameter is premised, is interpreted very broadly by the Functional Grammarians and embraces not only clearly visible physical movements but also any small difference capable of being perceived by any senses, including what Dowty (1979) refers to as 'indefinite change'. Furthermore, along with non-prototypical physical change, mental change too can be construed as representing 'dynamic' state of affairs.

Subsequently, the parameter of 'control' enters as a highly relevant factor which determines the grammatical treatment of agency in the FG framework. As argued in Chapter 2, a strong correlation has been recognised between the notions of 'control' and 'intentionality'/'awareness of action', which is an indispensable 'ingredient' of the agency concept. The lines below from Thalberg (1972:66) will remind the readers of this connection:

(12)   But more important is the extra-linguistic tie between awareness and control. Normally, the episodes we count as a person's intentional actions, and hence as being under his control, are also events of which he is aware – often without observation.

In fact, as Siewierska (1993:7) argues, 'control' is viewed as presupposing 'intentionality' in the FG model of state of affairs. What makes the functional approach to state of affairs even more attractive is that the notion of 'control' in the FG framework is premised on that of animacy as a defining factor, along with intentionality and sentiency (cf. Siewierska 1991 and 1993).

It should be borne in mind that the 'Functionalists' following the Fillmorean tradition of Case Grammar are by no means unanimous in their view on the conceptual features of agency; Dowty (1991), for instance, disregards animacy as one of the parameters determining the 'Proto-Agentive' role. However, it is 'the animacy hierarchy' which explains "the semantic naturalness for a lexically-specified noun phrase to function as agent of a true transitive verb, and inversely the naturalness of functioning as patient of such" (Silverstein 1976:113), and, conversely, "the association of the extended animacy hierarchy with case marking – high animacy with subjects and low animacy with objects – was first explained in terms of natural agency" (Croft 2003:179).[2]

On the grounds of the typology of SoAs as outlined so far, Dik (1989:101) distinguishes five 'nuclear' semantic roles, which may be borne by the first argument of a clause:

(13)   a.   Agent: the entity controlling an Action (= Activity or Accomplishment)
        b.   Positioner: the entity controlling a Position
        c.   Force: the non-controlling entity instigating a Process (= Dynamism or Change)
        d.   Processed: the entity that undergoes a Process
        e.   Zero (ø): the entity primarily involved in a State

The italicised noun phrases in (14) below exemplify these semantic roles (Dik 1989:101):

(14)   a.   *John* was reading a book. (Agent)
        b.   *John* kept his money in an old sock. (Positioner)
        c.   *The earthquake* moved the rock. (Force)

    d. *The rock* moved. (Processed)

    e. *The cup* was on the table. (ø)

An Agent is an animate entity who/which is granted a faculty of controlling an Action, such as *John* in *John was reading a book*, whereas a Force is an inanimate entity (or abstract entity) which does not have control of an Event whilst possessing the power to change the world to a certain extent. As Simon Dik (1989:101) himself acknowledges, the function of 'force' was first introduced by Huddleston (1970), and this dichotomy between the concepts of 'Agent' and 'Force' provides the fairly clear framework for the forthcoming case study in Japanese and English, although their boundary can sometimes be blurred by the metaphorical encoding of inferred animacy.

However, as mentioned earlier, even this grammatical device is not entirely problem-free. First and foremost, it must be noted that only 'first arguments' can be assigned the semantic role of 'Agent' in the above-mentioned framework, and it naturally follows that, 'passive agents' are regarded not as 'arguments' but as 'satellites' (Yamamoto 1999:175), since they are not obligatory constituents of predicates (Dik 1989:72–73). This treatment of granting only the first argument in a clause the faculty of agency can be somewhat controversial, but, for the sake of simplicity, our primary concern in the current project will be restricted to first arguments, when embarking upon the analysis of the Japanese-English parallel corpora.

Two other potential problems are with the above definition of the nuclear semantic roles/functions for the first arguments of a clause. As has been pointed out earlier, Fillmore's definition of the agentive case is not 100% congruous to the philosophical definition of agency, in that Fillmore's expression 'instigator' suggests the sense of 'causation' (or 'causality'). The same is true with Dik's definition of 'Force' above; a Force, being the non-controlling entity instigating a Process, is supposed to 'cause' the Event in question.

Secondly, the importance of the agency concept was to be stressed more strongly in the FG framework, if it handled the conceptual opposition between 'agency' and 'undergoing',[3] which has been popularly understood as the converse of agency (see Klaiman 1991:113; cf. also the opposition between 'Proto-Agent' and 'Proto-Patient' proposed by Dowty 1991). According to Klaiman, 'agency' and its counterpart, 'undergoing', are concepts much discussed in linguistics, but their origins are not in the tradition of grammatical theory but, once again, in Aristotle's discussion on the primacy of object *vs.* action. Although Dik assumes that 'Agent' takes the first position in the semantic function hierarchy (1989:232), the articulation of its direct foil could also articulate the primary status of agency in deciding the functional roles given to a first argument entity.

Another possible flaw of the FG classification of functions given to arguments seems to lie in the terminology referring to the roles listed in (13). Particularly awkward is the term 'Zero'; it is misleading that this term may be suggestive of an 'elliptical site', especially when it is accompanied with the sign 'ø', whilst the semantic role Zero can actually be borne by a noun phrase referring to an entity which *does* exist (at least linguistically). In the rest of this book, the sign 'ø' will be used quite frequently, but it designates ellipsis in any case, but not the semantic role of 'Zero' in the FG sense.

Along with the potential shortcomings of the FG interpretation of semantic roles, it also seems sensible to consider a couple of borderline cases regarding the attribution of agency to particular kinds of entities in a clause. In the Functionalist framework, the roles which are closest to the 'Agent' role are 'Positioner' and 'Force' in terms of 'dynamicity' and 'control', and, quite naturally, some Positioners and Forces bear more Agent-like propensities than others. For example, consider the following sentence from Siewierska (1991:68):

(15)   *The Indians* remained in the jungle.

Siewierska argues that *the Indians* in (15) is a typical example of the role of Positioner, which presupposes the faculty of control, but is not involved in any dynamicity or change; however, taking into account of 'mental change' which has been discussed earlier, *the Indians* can be a fairly good example of an Agent, if, for instance, they have decided to stay in the forest after a series of long debates. In fact, even if such subtle cases as above involving the result of certain mental processes are excluded, our philosophical interpretation of agency established in Chapter 2 can still accommodate many instances of animate 'Positioners' in the domain of agency, as far as they intentionally occupy certain 'Positions' or are aware of what they are 'doing' to occupy such 'Positions'.

'Forces' possess the power to change the world in one way or another, and the most prototypical entities which may bear this role include 'natural agents' previously discussed after Cruse (1973), as well as machines and organisations, which originally consist of a mass of human beings but are not animate themselves. However, as Siewierska (1991:69) points out, this role can be the function of the first argument of 'unintended actions' performed by animate beings, as *John* and *I* in the following sentences:

(16)   a.   *John* spilled the beer.
        b.   *I* accidentally tore the cover.

Despite several potential theoretical and terminological shortcomings and some borderline cases that demonstrate the haziness of the boundaries between certain roles, the FG treatment of state of affairs is still congruent to our philosophical definition of agency and hence will be adopted in the following section as appropriate grammatical machinery. The actual manifestations of the 'Agent' role as defined above will be investigated making use of the Japanese and English corpora. Choosing all the animate noun phrases in the parallel texts as the potential candidates of 'Agents' is a first step in the right direction, and then the likelihood of such animate entities being 'Agents' in Japanese and English corpora will be contrasted, yielding some interesting numerical arguments.

3.3 Manifestations of agency and impersonality in Japanese and English

3.3.1 Expression *vs.* suppression of agency: A hypothetical view

3.3.1.1 *Contrast between the two languages*
To start with, let me quote the famous lines in the classical piece of work by Leonard Bloomfield:

> (17)   Quite a few of the present-day Indo-European languages agree with English
>   in using an actor-action form as a favorite sentence-type. Some, such as the
>   other Germanic languages and French, agree also in that the actor-action form
>   is always a phrase, with the actor and the action as separate words or phrases.
>   .... Some languages have different favorite sentence-types.
>
> (Bloomfield 1933:172)

As Bloomfield (1933:172–175, 184) and many other linguists have pointed out, the favourite sentence construction type in the English language is an 'actor-action' form, in which an animate entity tends to be highlighted as an 'instigator' of an action, testifying to a general tendency observed in a wide range of Indo-European languages. (Notice that, in Bloomfield's terminology, an 'actor' is used in the same way as an 'agent'.)

Bloomfield also acknowledged, as stated in the above quotation, that some other languages have different favourite sentence types. In Japanese, by contrast, the favourite sentence construction type is an 'event' form, where the existence of agents, who/which are mostly animate beings, and their voluntary actions are often submerged in the whole course of an 'event' described by a particular sentence (Andō 1986; Ikegami 1981, 1982 and 1991; Yamamoto 1999).[4] Strictly speaking, this characterisation of English and Japanese does not obtain in a philosophical sense, since 'actions' constitute a subclass of 'events' (see, for example, Davidson 1971; Thalberg 1972). The expression 'event' the linguists speak of here must be interpreted as a more general, pretheoretical concept; in the following discussion, this terminological distinction between the rigorously philosophical concept of 'event' and the term 'event' in an everyday sense will often remain quite fuzzy.

In the last section of Chapter 2, it was argued that 'animacy' is the most fundamental conceptual constituent of 'agency', with other constituents such as 'intentionality' and 'awareness of action' falling into the domain of 'inferred animacy', and that the agency concept captures the most animate-like aspect of animate beings. The manifestations of animacy in the two languages in question have already been analysed statistically (Yamamoto 1999), and the conclusion clearly drawn from my previous research was that animacy is articulately expressed in English, whereas its verbal manifestation is considerably suppressed in the act of reference in Japanese; this obtains in regard to both the Hierarchy of Persons and the Individuation Scale, the parameters which intersect with the main General Animacy Scale as defined in Section 2.5.

The expression used above "its [of animacy] verbal manifestation is considerably suppressed in the act of reference in Japanese" suggests that in many cases the entities possibly conveying strong animacy may not be overtly expressed in words but often undergo ellipsis in Japanese, and this is the case in both written and spoken texts. 'Nothingness' encodes neither animacy nor agency verbally, thus impersonalising the action or event in question. Several examples of Japanese ellipses can be found in the following texts:

(18)   Ø   *Kōcha*   *ga*   *nomi-tai.*
       (I:NOM) English:tea ACC drink-want:to
       '(I) want to have (some) tea'.

(19) a. "... *asoko ja rokusuppo* Ø   *hanashi mo deki-nai shi,*
       "... there in properly   (we:NOM) talk   ACC can-NEG and,
       Ø   *sangai   no ongaku kissa o* Ø   *oshie-toita   no*".
       (I:NOM) third:floor LK music café ACC (her:DAT) show-PERF".
                                          (Yukio Mishima, *Hyaku-man Yen Sembei*)

    b. "But it's too noisy to talk there, and *I* told *her* about the music coffee shop on the third floor instead".
                                          (English translation of the above by E. G. Seidensticker)

(20) CHIBA: Ø   *Oboete-nai*   *nā.*
            (I:NOM) Remember-NEG.
            '(I) don't remember'.

    TSUTSUMI: Ø   *Itsumo Shōnen Raidā-tai   ni, kakom-are*
              (You:TOP) Always Boys'   Rider-club by surround-PASS
              tei-ta   noni   desu ka?
              PROG-PAST although COP QU?
              'Although (you) have been always surrounded by the Boys' Rider Club?'

    SASAKI: Ø   *Wakareru toki ni* "*Taichō,   mata kaette   kite*
            (You:NOM) Separating time at "Captain, again return   come

kudasai" tte   iw-are-te-ta   noni,   Jirō-chan
please"   that tell-PASS-PROG-PAST although, Jirō-chan

hontoni hakujō-nan dakara!
really   heartless   COP!
'Although (you) were told "Please come back", ... Jirō-chan (you)
was (were) really a bastard!'   (Takeshi Sasaki, *Ichimonji Hayato*)

(21) a. Ø   *Shitagawa-nai to* Ø   *zōbin*   o
          (They:NOM) Obey-NEG   if (he:NOM) increase:of:flight ACC
          mitome-nai to, Ø   *seisai-sochi made chiratsukase-ta.*
          permit-NEG that, (he:NOM) sanction   even flash-PAST.
                                              (*Asahi Shimbun*, 22 September 1994)

     b. *He* went so far as to threaten JAL with sanctions saying that if the carrier
         did not comply with his instruction, *he* would not authorize an increase
         in the number of JAL flights.
         (English translation of the above in *Asahi Evening News*, 22 September
         1994)

The examples in (18) to (21) illustrate the wide-spread use of ellipsis as a means
of first, second and third person references.[5] As we have seen earlier, English also
avoids the use of first and second person reference in order to obfuscate agency
(cf. Section 2.4), but, in the case of Japanese, the dominance of ellipsis (or zero
anaphora[6]) does not seem to stem only from the face threatening effects potentially
caused by direct reference to referents. Third person reference too is made most
exclusively by ellipsis in Japanese (Yamamoto 1999: 118–125), and this is largely
due to the generally observed reluctance to employ a group of nouns which are
regarded as equivalent to personal pronouns in European languages (and they are
actually categorised as 'personal pronouns' by most grammarians)[7] but are sensitive to the formality of speech events and the gender of the speakers, addressees
and referents, unlike their equivalents in European languages.

Japanese preference for ellipsis over personal pronouns suggests that the
speakers and writers of this language tend to express human beings (particularly
human agents which are most likely to be subjects of a clause) by means of impersonal 'nothingness', instead of referring to them by means of very personal
information encoded by personal pronouns. The prevalence of 'nothingness' and
'impersonality' or 'impersonalness' in the Japanese language arouses intriguing arguments. 'Impersonality' designates an impersonal nuance brought about by the
non-agentive styles of expressing actions and events, and impersonality phenomena in Japanese are caused not only by ellipsis but, as we shall see in this chapter,
by means of a series of periphrastic person referential expressions, which do not
encode strong animacy and agency, as well as impersonal clause constructions. In
Chapter 4, we will come back to the Japanese preference of impersonal expressions

and shall further investigate its socio-cultural background. Before then, we need to observe more examples of the Japanese ways of agent effacement, as compared with the English willingness to overtly express human agency, and elicit certain linguistic principles which can explain the gradience concerning the strength of encoding agency.

3.3.1.2 *Even a terrorist may lose his agency*

'Terrorism', which is doubtless our uttermost concern these days, has also been one of the most 'agentive' human activities in the modern world. Ten years ago, one of the most wanted terrorists of the time was captured in France; his name was Illich Ramírez Sanchez, internationally renowned as 'Carlos the Jackal', who was extremely successful in his career as a terrorist and used to enjoy luxurious life occupying a corner of a prestigious hotel and driving a fancy car. When this world-famous terrorist of Venezuelan origin was eventually arrested by the French secret services, the media reported the simple fact about the change in his life, as in:

(22)   Carlos began his new life at La Santé prison in Paris.

(Newsweek, 29 August 1994)

The above sentence was quoted from *Newsweek*, but the Japanese edition of the same magazine presented the same fact in quite a different way:

(23)   *Kōshite, Karurosu no   na   de shira-reru   kokusai   terorisuto*
       Thus,   Carlos   GEN name by know-PART international terrorist
       no   Pari no Sante keimusho deno seikatsu ga   hajima-tta.
       GEN Paris in Santé prison   at life   NOM begin-PAST.
       'Thus, the life of the international terrorist known as "Carlos" began at La Santé prison in Paris'.   (*Newsweek* (Japanese edition), 31 August 1994)

What is the major difference between the way in which clauses (22) and (23) express the same incident? On the one hand, the former, i.e. a sentence in the original English edition, describes the action (or 'Action' in Simon Dik's terms) of the ex-terrorist, Carlos, being depicted as a human agent fully aware of having to begin his 'new life'; on the other hand, in the corresponding Japanese clause, the whole situation is expressed as an actionless and rather impersonal event or, under a different guise, a 'Process' as Functional Grammarians would call it.

In (23) extracted from the Japanese edition of *Newsweek*, Carlos' new life simply 'began', with no reference to and without regard to the agency of the man himself. In other words, the same human entity, Carlos, is expressed in terms of two completely different grammatical elements: he is an 'Agent' in the English clause in (22), while he is not even an 'argument' in the Japanese clause in (23). The non-argument genitive noun phrases in the above Japanese example, *Karurosu no* ('of Carlos') and *terorisuto no* ('of (the) terrorist') with the postpositional particle *no* signifying a genitive case, are certainly too weak and impersonal grammatical devices to highlight the protagonist, but, at least, the existence of Carlos is not completely 'effaced' by means of ellipsis here.

Below is another set of interesting examples, which have been referred to in Chapter 1:

(24) a.   *Nichiyōbi   heiten.*
            Sunday   closed:shop.
       b.   We are closed on Sundays.   (Ikegami 1982:90)

As we have observed in the Introduction, the examples in (24a) and (24b) are messages in Japanese and English to inform the customers that the shop is closed on Sundays. The Japanese expression in (24a) does not present a fully-fledged clause (or sentence) structure: it has no human subject, but it is not because the subject underwent ellipsis unlike the examples we have seen in (18)–(21). As the human subject (agent) is missing from the beginning, the resulting phrase sounds highly impersonal, and it is natural that no one can tell who is instigating an intentional action of closing the shop. Indeed, (24a) designates an entirely impersonal event. In (24b), however, the corresponding English sentence (which possesses a fully-fledged sentence structure, unlike its Japanese counterpart) saliently expresses the people – the proprietor and/or the shop attendants – who are responsible for closing this shop on Sundays. It is the personal pronoun *we* that clearly signals the intentional human action, although, on a surface grammatical level, *we* in (24b) cannot be classified as an 'Agent'.

One of the very interesting findings of the investigation into the parallel Japanese and English corpora, whose details will be introduced later, is that an English 'Agentive' noun phrase sometimes corresponds to a Japanese non-Agentive, inanimate expression, which gives the whole clause a strong flavour of 'impersonality'. One such case can be observed in (25) below:

(25) a.   *Karuban Kurain ni "Kenedī   jaketto" toyū na   no futatsu*
            Calvin   Klein   at "Kennedy jacket"   that name LK two
            botan   no burezā ga   chanto aru.
            button   LK blazer NOM   readily exist.
                                      (*Newsweek* (Japanese edition), 7 September 1994)
       b.   Of course, every Jackie needs a Jack, so Calvin Klein's less-expensive CK menswear line includes a two-button blazer that <u>he</u>'s dubbed "the Kennedy jacket".   (*Newsweek*, 29 August 1994)

In the Japanese translational text in (25a), on the one hand, Calvin Klein (or *Karuban Kurain* in a Japanese way of pronunciation) is treated as an apparel company *where* one can buy 'the Kennedy jacket', with the postposition *ni* (translated as 'at' in the word-for-word translation) signifying a location. On the other hand, in the original English version of *Newsweek* in (25b), Calvin Klein is expressed as an individual designer who named his two-button blazer as 'the Kennedy jacket'. In (25b), it is clear, as the underline shows, that *he* referring to Calvin Klein himself is the Agent of the relative clause modifying *a two-button blazer* (Yamamoto 1999:144). As it will be argued later in this chapter, such cases that an English Agent corresponds to a Japanese non-Agentive expression are commonly found in the corpus data.

The predominant style of encoding agency seems different from language to language, and the difference can be explained in terms of the gradience between the two contrary tendencies of highlighting and obfuscating the concept of agency (and that of animacy which is presupposed by agency) (Yamamoto 1999:159). Ikegami (1982 and 1991) proposes the following 'hypothesis' concerning these two extreme tendencies in connection to the perception of the salience of human and agentive entities involved in certain events:

> (26)   There is a contrast between (1) a language which focuses on 'the human being (especially, one acting as agent)' and tends to give linguistic prominence to the notion [of agency] and (2) a language which tends to suppress the notion of 'the human being (especially, one acting as agent)', even if such a being is involved in the event.   (Ikegami 1991:290)

It is evident from our previous discussions that English exhibits a strong tendency for the first mode of treating agency, and that Japanese for the second: English tends to overtly accentuate Agents, whilst Japanese is reluctant to verbalise Agentive elements, covering up their prominence by means of ellipsis and the impersonal organisation of propositions.

Ikegami's argument above should be regarded not merely as a 'hypothesis' but as one of the most striking facts about the two languages in question, which reveals a great deal about the 'epistemic attitudes' or 'mind-styles' of their speakers. The next subsection will elucidate the 'fact' in more detail by making use of clear-cut data acquired through the analysis of the corpus. Our emphasis will be upon those entities in English texts which are both animate (human) and agentive and their corresponding Japanese expressions which are neither animate (human) nor agentive to observe the clearest and possibly the most extreme contrast between articulating and inhibiting the expression of agency in the two languages.

3.3.2 Analysis of agency in Japanese/English corpus

3.3.2.1 *Nature of data*

The 18th century Scottish empiricist philosopher, David Hume, once argued the importance of abstract reasoning concerning quantity and number and bitterly criticised his contemporaries whose works did not contain any numerical data,

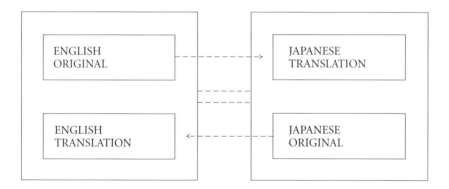

Figure 1. Structure of Japanese-English parallel corpus (cf. Yamamoto 1999:85)

demanding that such volumes 'should be committed to the flames'. To ensure the objectivity of the following discussions, a quantitative analysis of Japanese and English texts has been made, utilising 'parallel corpora'[8] of the two languages and yielding some significant statistical results, so that Hume would not have wished to commit this book to the flames.

Although it is not the central concern in the current context, a brief description of the corpus data that I have used as a basis of the later argument must be provided here. The Japanese-English parallel corpus, whose structure is schematised above in Figure 1, consists of both (1) texts originally written in Japanese and their English translations and (2) those originally written in English and their Japanese translations. It should be noted that the translational texts (in both Japanese and English) are basically free translations which are published in the form of books or articles.

The most significant benefit of using the bi-directional translation corpus (as indicated by the arrows in the above figure) is that it can mitigate the effect of 'translationese', that is, deviance in translated texts induced by the source language (Johansson & Hofland 1994:26).

The parallel corpora, that I have used for this statistical survey into the linguistic manifestations of agency in Japanese and English, consist of six different types of written texts, covering quite a wide range of genres.[9] Texts 1 and 2 are literary texts, Texts 3 and 4 comprise pieces of journalistic language and Texts 5 and 6 are scientific writing. The sources of these are as follows:

(27) Text 1 (Japanese original and English translation):
      Yukio Mishima, *Hyaku-man Yen Sembei* ('One Million Yen Rice Crackers') and its translation by Edward G. Seidensticker entitled *Three Million Yen*.

      Text 2 (English original and Japanese translation):
      Agatha Christie, *Murder on the Orient Express* and its translation by Tadae Fukisawa.

Text 3 (Japanese original and English translation):
Editorials in *Asahi Shimbun* and their translations in *Asahi Evening News*.

Text 4 (English original and Japanese translation):
Articles in *Newsweek* (English and Japanese editions).

Text 5 (Japanese original and English translation):
Articles in *The Transactions of the Institute of Electronics, Information and Communication Engineers* and their English translations in *Systems and Computers in Japan*.

Text 6 (English original and Japanese translation):
Articles in *Scientific American* (English and Japanese editions).

Some extracts from Texts 1, 3 and 4 have already been examined above in (19), (21), (22), (23) and (25).

It seems quite important to collect texts from a variety of different genres, since each genre may characteristically exhibit particular syntactic patterns. Hence, investigating only one type of text may result in a biased generalisation. For instance, in the Japanese translation of Agatha Christie's *Murder on the Orient Express* (Text 2), a number of personal pronouns can be found reflecting the characteristics of the original English version, whereas the use of personal pronouns is severely restricted in other types of written (and spoken) discourse in Japanese. However, relatively frequent use of personal pronouns is not untypical of Japanese translation of Western literature, and we can argue that this is a good example of 'translationese'. Another area which we need to be careful about is English scientific writing (Text 6). It seems to be generally the case that scientific texts in English are prone to 'agentless' passives without reference to human/animate entities. However, as obvious from our previous discussions, this by no means suggests that English is a language which tends to avoid reference to human agents.

From each of the texts listed above, 300 animate (mostly human) noun phrases, who/which (according to our argument in Chapter 2) can be potential agents of certain actions, have been picked up; this means that we will be listing 1,800 animate and potentially agentive expressions in both Japanese and English texts altogether. My basic policy of analysing the parallel corpus data is to carefully observe the correspondence between the actual Japanese and English expressions with the same reference in the same context. It is particularly interesting to study the cases where a particular English expression has no corresponding form in the Japanese text, or vice versa, our attention focussed upon those entities in English texts which are animate (human) and agentive and their corresponding Japanese expressions which are neither animate (human) nor agentive that highlight the contrast between the suppression and articulation of agency in Japanese and English.

3.3.2.2 *Numerical discussions and analysis of examples*

As has already been argued following Bloomfield's typological insight, the above-mentioned contrast between the expression and obfuscation of agency can be partly ascribed to the structural difference between the two languages, the favourite clausal constructions in Japanese and English being an 'event' pattern and an 'actor-action' pattern respectively.[10] On the other hand, even in 'actor-action' clauses, the absence of agentive entities can be caused by ellipsis; theoretically, this can be the case in both Japanese and English, but in the overwhelmingly majority of cases, the effacement of agency in 'actor-action form' clauses is observed in the former. In other words, it could be argued that ellipsis can resolve the 'actor-action' pattern of clause construction into the impersonal and seemingly 'event form' structure and imbue it with the sense of impersonality. The straightforward numerical discussion below, utilising a relatively small body of both Japanese and English texts, will clearly illustrate either of the cases described above.

First of all, the predominance of ellipsis as a means of person reference in Japanese has been observed in the figures obtained through the analysis of the above-mentioned corpora; in Texts 1 to 6 (with 300 animate entities in each text), the number of ellipsis is 465, forming 25.83% of a total of 1,800 items. The manifestations of ellipsis in English texts (Texts 1 to 6) add up only to 7 out of 1,800, which forms 0.39% of the total number. The number of the occurrence of ellipsis in the English corpus constitutes only 1.5% of the number of ellipsis found in the corresponding Japanese texts (cf. Yamamoto 1999: 163).

Secondly, an inanimate/impersonal and non-Agentive expression in Japanese texts may substitute for a possible animate and Agentive expression in the corresponding English texts, and vice versa, as exemplified in (25) above which has been extracted from Text 4 of the parallel corpora. Lastly, in a piece of parallel corpus, there can be no referential expression at all in one language corresponding to an entity verbally encoded in the other language.

The statistics provided below in Tables 1 and 2 are based on the analysis of only the literary and journalistic texts in the parallel corpora, that is, Texts 1 to 4 (cf. Yamamoto 1999: 164–165). As I have argued earlier, the scientific texts, particularly pieces of English scientific writing extracted from *Scientific American* (Text 6), require special caution: what is unusually problematic with scientific texts in English is that they abound in 'agentless' passives without reference to any human (animate) and Agentive entities, although, of course, this does not mean that the English language in general tends to avoid reference to human agents. As Cruse (1973) demonstrated, the agency concept is concerned with not only the nature of noun phrases but also that of verb phrases or, more precisely, states of affairs expressed by predicates. The data taken from the scientific texts in the corpora (Texts 5 and 6) had to be abandoned, since the variety of states of affairs dealt with therein is severely limited to that which does not make reference to human agency.

Table 1. Japanese non-Agents corresponding to English Agents

	Number	%
Ellipsis	80	52.63%
Inanimate/non-Agentive alternatives	8	5.26%
No corresponding expressions	64	42.11%
Total	152	

Table 2. English non-Agents corresponding to Japanese Agents

	Number	%
Ellipsis	0	0.00%
Inanimate/non-Agentive alternatives	3	60.00%
No corresponding expressions	2	40.00%
Total	5	

As shown in Table 1, the number of cases where the Japanese texts have no Agentive (and animate) entities corresponding to the Agentive noun phrases in the English texts is 152, which adds up to 12.67% of the total of 1,200 items under observation. Inversely, Table 2 illustrates that the cases where Japanese Agentive entities have no Agentive (and animate) equivalents in the English texts occurred only 5 times; this figure forms only 0.42% of the total of 1,200 cases. Clearly, there are (slightly more than) 30 times more instances of the Japanese non-Agentive and inanimate items for English Agents than those of the English non-Agentive/inanimate entities corresponding to Japanese Agents. Moreover, the number of Japanese 'missing slots' occupies more than one eighth of the entire list of (potential) human/animate referential expressions found in Texts 1 to 4.

Although the size of the parallel corpora is relatively small, the figures attained through the above case study eloquently support the salient opposition between the obfuscation of agency in Japanese and its overt articulation in English. What can be further observed behind the numerical discussions above? The rest of this subsection will be devoted for the 'qualitative' assessment of the data obtained through the corpora. More than half of the cases of the contrast between Japanese 'nothingness' of some measure (including 'inanimate/non-Agentive alternatives') *vs.* English Agents are caused by ellipsis, which is quite predictable. As stated earlier, ellipsis is the most 'unmarked' means of person reference in Japanese, and it breaks the 'actor-action' pattern of clause construction, thus functioning as a prevailing device to avoid the explicit encoding of agency and to impersonalise human actions.

Here are some examples, where the correspondence between English Agents and Japanese elliptical sites can be observed (the relevant expressions are undelined):

(28) a. "<u>Ø</u>   *Sonna fū   ni o-kangae-ninatte wa   dame   yo....*"
          "<u>(You:NOM)</u> Such   way in think-HON   TOP no:good COP...."
                                          (Text 2: Japanese translation of the below)

      b. "Oh! <u>You</u> mustn't think that...."
                                    (Text 2: Agatha Christie, *Murder on the Orient Express*)

(29) a. <u>Ø</u>   *Muryō bīru pātī, pai gui   kyōsō, jiruba*
          <u>(They:NOM)</u> Free   beer party, pie eat:ing race, jittering
          kontesuto ... nado de   Ø   "seikō"   o   iwat-ta.
          contest ...   etc.   with (their:GEN) "success" ACC celebrate-PAST.
                                          (Text 3: *Asahi Shimbun*, 18 September 1994)

      b. <u>The Americans</u> celebrated their "success" with a free beer party, pie-
          eating race, jittering contest ... and other activities.
          (Text 3: *Asahi Evening News* (English translation of the above), 25
          September 1994)

(30) a. <u>Ø</u>   *Kore-made ni 83-nin   no inochi o   ubat-ta   to*
          <u>(He:NOM)</u> Until-this to 83-people GEN life   ACC rob-PAST that
          sare-teiru   ga, ...
          suppose:PASS-ing but, ...
                                          (Text 4: *Newsweek* (Japanese edition), 31 August 1994)

      b. <u>He</u> allegedly killed 83 people, but ...
                                          (Text 4: *Newsweek*, 29 August 1994)

(31) a. "... <u>Ø</u>   *Sangai   no ongaku kissa o   Ø*
          "... <u>(I:NOM)</u> Third:floor LK music   café ACC (her:DAT)
          oshie-toita no".
          show-PERF".
                                          (Text 1: Yukio Mishima, *Hyaku-man Yen Sembei*)

      b. "... and <u>I</u> told her about the music coffee shop on the third floor instead".
                                          (Text 1: English translation of the above)

In the examples (28) to (31), all Japanese and English clauses that contain the
underlined noun phrases take the form of an 'actor-action' pattern, and their state
of affairs can be classified as 'Actions' which are both [+ dynamic] and [+ control]
in Simon Dik's terms. In the Japanese texts, the potential Agents are not encoded
verbally, hence making the existence of human agents blurred and the entire clause
construction look impersonal and (possibly) somewhat incomplete.

   Another interpretation is that an elliptical 'actor-action' clause may not be
incomplete, but should instead be regarded simply as an 'action' clause without
an 'actor'. Since 'action' constitutes a subclass of 'event', as argued in Chapter 2,
following Aristotle, such 'action' clauses may naturally be classified as a variant of
'event' clauses. The identities of the participants acting in such 'action' (or 'event')
clauses are easily recoverable from the context in the above Japanese extracts, and

no potential ambiguity arises. If the missing slots in (28)–(31) were to be filled with explicit Agents by means of personal pronouns, for instance, such as *anata* ('you'), *kare-ra* ('they'), *kare* ('he')[11] and *watashi* ('I') respectively, the resulting forms may sound both redundant and pretty 'affected'.[12]

In other cases, the equivalent of an English Agentive noun phrase may be a Japanese elliptical site that is not a part of a clause in the 'actor-action' form. In (32a) below, for example, it should be noted not only that the performer of the (potential) action undergoes ellipsis, but that the 'action' itself is deprived of dynamicity and the performer's control over it, the state of affairs involved being not that of 'Action' but that of 'State' in the terminology of Functional Grammar. The absence of a human actor and the conversion of 'Action' into 'State' considerably impersonalise the entire clause.

(32) a. "Ø̲   *Sutanbūru ni wa   sūjisu   go-tōryū   no*
          "(You:TOP) Stamboul in TOP few:days HON-sojourn LK
          go-yotei   de-gozaimasu ka?"
          HON-schedule   COP-HON   QU?"
                                    (Text 2: Japanese translation of the below)

      b. "And y̲o̲u̲ intend to remain there [in Stamboul] a few days, I̲ ̲t̲h̲i̲n̲k̲?"
                          (Text 2: Agatha Christie, *Murder on the Orient Express*)

The inverse (and direct) English translation of the Japanese clause in (32a) is something like: "(As for you), in Stamboul (Istanbul), is a few day's stay the (your) schedule?" Whilst the English original highlights the intentionality of the Agent, the Japanese translation expresses the entire State as if it is an established fact without regard to the addressee's spontaneous intentionality (Yamamoto 1999: 167) and with a strong sense of impersonality. The other interesting feature of the above extract is that the last clause of the English original that is marked by a wavy line is not translated into Japanese but simply omitted. It is an 'actor-action' clause with 'I' as an Agent, which has no equivalent expression whatsoever in the corresponding Japanese text.

As illustrated in Table 1, 8 cases have been observed where English Agentive noun phrases have inanimate (and naturally non-Agentive) expressions as their counterparts, which are not elliptical, but encoded verbally. Two of such instances are shown below:

(33) a. *Kore ni taishite* R̲o̲s̲h̲i̲a̲-̲g̲a̲w̲a̲ *wa   senshū   hajime,   kengi*
          This to against R̲u̲s̲s̲i̲a̲n̲-̲s̲i̲d̲e̲ NOM last:week beginning, suspicion
          o   tsuyoku hitei.
          ACC   strongly deny.
                          (Text 4: *Newsweek* (Japanese edition), 31 August 1994)

b. Early last week <u>the Russians</u> hotly denied that the rogue plutonium was theirs.   (Text 4: *Newsweek*, 29 August 1994)

(34) a. [*Kurinton seiken*   *ga*   *mizukara*   *seoikon-da*]   *seiji*
          [<u>Clinton administration</u> NOM   voluntarily   shoulder-PART]   political
          kadai
          problem
                                    (Text 3: *Asahi Shimbun*, 20 September 1994)

b. a political problem [that <u>President Clinton himself</u> stepped forward to tackle in the first place]
    (Text 3: *Asahi Evening News* (the English translation of the above), 20 September 1994)

Extract (33) illustrates a good example of an impersonality phenomenon. The Japanese noun phrase *Roshia-gawa* ('Russian side') in (33a) does not refer to individual human beings, but suggests a certain political 'position' of the entire nation (Yamamoto 1999: 168) – we will come back to this specific instance in the following chapter, as it is a typical manifestation of an 'impersonalised' proposition containing an example of what can be termed as 'positionalisation (or locationalisation) of persons' (cf. Yamamoto 1992b; Ikegami 1991). The expression *Roshia-gawa* ('Russian side') is an inanimate noun phrase in itself, but belongs to the 'borderline cases' between the animates and inanimates discussed in Section 2.5, since the nation 'Russia' is a 'local community' or a 'geographical entity' which signifies a 'body of individual human beings' on an extremely large scale. The corresponding English clause in (33b) articulates the 'hot' agency of *the Russians* – at least some Russians in the government who possibly knew something about the nuclear threat.

There is also an interesting contrast between the relative clauses in (34a) and (34b) (marked with square brackets) which modify the noun phrases *seiji kadai* or *a political problem* (note that a Japanese relative clause precedes a noun phrase that it qualifies). Whilst the Japanese clause encapsulates the 'Process' as if the decision has been made collectively and hence impersonally, employing an inanimate 'Force', *Kurinton seiken* ('Clinton administration'), its English counterpart intensifies the agency and responsibility of Mr. Clinton as an individual 'Agent', with the reflexive pronoun *himself* accompanying the Agentive noun phrase *President Clinton*.

It can also be observed from Table 1 that, in 64 cases, English Agentive items have no equivalent noun phrases whatsoever in the corresponding Japanese texts. The principal reason for the structural loss of Japanese Agentive expressions seems to be that, as illustrated above through Ikegami's (1991) argument, Japanese tends to construct a clause without granting an animate entity a 'privileged' status as an Agent, i.e. without dissecting a proposition into an 'actor' and an 'action' in

Bloomfield's (1933) terms, as many European languages including English do (Yamamoto 1999). In (35b) below, for example, the original English clause extracted from *Newsweek* dissects the event (more precisely, the Action) into the actor or the Agent, *German officials*, and what they did, i.e. confiscating the dangerous, radioactive commodities. The corresponding Japanese translational clause in (35a), however, expresses the same event in the form of a very impersonal Process in quite a different way with no reference at all to the agency of the German officials. Simply, the confiscation of plutonium and uranium took place in Germany for three times, and it does not matter who made the seizure.

(35)   a.   *Doitsu de-wa*   *5-gatsu irai,   heiki   ni tenyō dekiru*
             Germany in-TOP May   since, weapon to divert can

             shōryō   no purutoniumu ya   uran   ga   hokani
             small:amount LK plutonium   and uranium NOM additionally

             3-kai   mo ōshū-sare-teiru.
             three-times   seize-PASS-PERF.
                                     (Text 4: *Newsweek* (Japanese edition), 31 August 1994)

       b.   Since May, German officials have made three other seizures of tiny amounts of weapons-grade plutonium and uranium.
                                     (Text 4: *Newsweek*, 29 August 1994)

Another example which clearly illustrates the opposition between the clause construction of the 'event pattern' and that of the 'actor-action pattern' in Japanese and English respectively can be observed in the extract (36) below. (36a) and (36b) reflect the completely different interpretations of the scene of a funfair and present an interesting contrast between the mind-styles of the two languages.

(36)   a.   "... *Kōyū tokoro wa,   hitotsu hitotsu wa   yasui yō   demo,*
             "... Such place TOP,   one   one   TOP cheap seem though,

             kekkyoku   omoigake-nai o-kane o   tsuka-waseru   yō-ni
             eventually unexpected money ACC spend-cause:PART as

             deki-teru   n-da-mono".
             made-PART COP".
                                     (Text 1: Yukio Mishima, *Hyaku-man Yen Sembei*)

       b.   "... Everything seems so cheap, but it's all arranged so that [you spend more money than you intend to]".
                                     (Text 1: English translation of the above)

In the original Japanese text, the speaker expresses her idea in terms of a Situation (more precisely, a State, which is [– control]) with a strong sense of impersonality as in: a funfair is simply arranged in such and such a way. Of course, there are people behind the scene who organise a funfair so that people spend more money than they expect and those who actually spend their money, but no sign of human agency and intentionality can be detected in the impersonal Situation or State in (36a). The corresponding English text in (36b), on the other hand, clearly marks the human agency of those who spend their money as expressed in an embedded clause (marked with square brackets), although the state of affairs in the main clause is that of a State, which describes how a funfair is arranged and does not reveal the hidden agency and intentionality of the organisers (cf. Section 2.4).

The generic use of the second person pronoun *you*, which encodes the agency of the (potential) customers in (36b), is also of a considerable analytical interest. Whilst the generic use of second person personal/possessive pronouns is quite a widespread phenomenon in English, none of such instances can be found in Japanese (Yamamoto 1999:Ch. 3). It can be argued that the favourite pattern of clause construction in English – i.e. an 'actor-action pattern' – is supported by the extensive use of generic personal pronouns; when the speaker/writer does not have a clear idea for the identity of a potential actor, the generic personal pronouns can function as 'dummy' Agents (Yamamoto 1999:170). Benjamin Lee Whorf, whose relativity hypothesis will be revisited in Chapter 4, pointed out the nature of English 'dummy' actors, arguing that "we are constantly reading into nature fictional acting entities", "because our verbs must have substantives in front of them" (1956:243), the 'substantive in front of a verb' meaning the 'actor' in the 'actor-action pattern' of clause formation.[13]

So far the focus of our attention has been upon the 'unmarked' cases where Agentive (and animate) noun phrases in the English texts do not have any Agentive (and animate) equivalents in the parallel Japanese texts. However, as has been illustrated in Table 2, 5 exceptional cases, where Japanese Agentive (and animate) noun phrases have no corresponding Agentive forms in the parallel English texts, have also been found in the parallel corpus data. The exceptions also need some explanations, and two examples are provided in (37) and (38) below:

(37) a. *Busshu-shi* wa *beikoku* o *mezasu* *Haichi* *nanmin* o
      Mr-Bush NOM America ACC head:PART Haitian refugee ACC
      kyōsei *sōkan* *shi-ta.*
      coercive deportation do-PAST.
      (Text 3: *Asahi Shimbun*, 20 September 1994)

   b. The Bush administration's policy was to return Haitian refugees who headed for the United States.
      (Text 3: *Asahi Evening News* (English translation of the above text), 20 September 1994)

Including the case shown in (37), where the Japanese Agentive expression *Busshu-shi* ('Mr. Bush') corresponds to the English noun phrase *The Bush administration*, the English texts in the parallel corpora exhibit 3 instances of inanimate (and hence non-Agentive) entities corresponding to Japanese Agents.[14] Although no instance of English ellipsis was found to correspond to Japanese Agentive noun phrases, there are also 2 cases of English 'nothingness' being equivalent to Japanese Agents in Texts 1 to 4, one of which is extracted in (38).

(38) a.   *Kono natsu   ryūkō no sodenashi wanpīsu   wa,* [*kanojo*
           This summer vogue LK sleeveless one:piece:dress TOP, she

           ga   Onashisu fujin dat-ta   koro aiyō-shi-ta]   *mono to*
           NOM Onassis   wife   COP-PAST when patronise-PART thing to

           sokkuri   da.
           very:similar COP.

                               (Text 4: *Newsweek* (Japanese edition), 7 September 1994)

      b.   The sleeveless shifts [women are wearing this summer] stepped right out
           of the Onassis years.   (Text 4: *Newsweek*, 29 August 1994)

The above example is taken from an article in *Newsweek* on the revival of the fashion *a la* Jacqueline Kennedy Onassis. In (38a), a rare[15] example of Japanese third person personal pronoun – *kanojo*, meaning 'she' – can be observed in a relative clause, which qualifies a noun *mono* ('thing') and is marked with square brackets. The direct (and reverse) English translation of this Japanese relative clause reads something like: "She [Jacqueline Kennedy Onassis], when (she) was Mrs. Onassis, loved to wear", and it is clear here that *kanojo* ('she') is the Agent of the clause. The original English text illustrates the same sleeveless shifts in vogue as the product of 'the Onassis years', without reference to Mrs. Onassis as a person; this contrast is the very reverse of the cases where English Agents have no equivalent animate/inanimate noun phrases in the corresponding Japanese texts, as observed in (25), (35) and (36).

Example (38), however, needs to be analysed more closely and yields further interesting discussions. In the English original text in (38b), there is another relative clause in square brackets, *women are wearing this summer*, with the generic noun phrase *women* as an Agent: the English text thereby finds a certain generic human agency in the fashion industry, which its Japanese equivalent does not encode. Secondly, the main clause in (38b) is of a significant rhetorical interest. According to Simon Dik's framework of semantic roles, the verb phrase "stepped right out of the Onassis years" is to be interpreted as manifesting a 'dynamic' state of affairs which is 'controlled' – most prototypically by an Agent. However, this clause has the *sleeveless shifts* as something like a 'metaphorical Force', which can be interpreted as syntactically 'personified'. The actor-action pattern of clause construction in English is so prevalent that even an inanimate object or abstract entities/concepts can be readily expressed as though it were an actor of some measure on a syntactic level (Yamamoto 1999: 171–172). Conversely, in the tradition of Japanese literature, where impersonal expression of events prevails and is commonly regarded as desireable, 'personification' is sometimes viewed quite unfavourably as a means of figurative speech (cf. Chamberlain 1939). These contrastive epistemic attitudes towards personification in the two languages will be brought into focus again in Chapter 5, which is a concluding chapter but will also serve as a 'waste-basket' in this book.

In concluding the current chapter, we will examine two more instances from the parallel Japanese and English corpora – one demonstrates a rather extreme case, and the other represents a widespread contrast between the two languages in question which has not been examined numerically in this chapter, but significantly fortifies our arguments so far.

(39) a. *"Fufu".*   (Text 1: Yukio Mishima, *Hyaku-man Yen Sembei*)
       b. Kenzo laughed.   (Text 1: English translation of the above)

The above set of examples illustrates a case where an English clause containing an Agentive entity does not have a semantically equivalent clause in a corresponding piece of Japanese text. Of remarkable interest is that the original Japanese expression in (39a) simply shows the way the protagonist laughed by means of an onomatopoeia, whereas its English translational clause follows the 'actor-action' pattern with *Kenzo* as a grammatical and semantic Agent. This example seems quite conspicuous for demonstrating that even one simple onomatopoeic word (which is inevitably impersonal) can convey the same amount of information in the Japanese language as that carried by a fully-fledged 'actor-action' sentence in English, let alone an 'event form' clause without an overt Agent.

Up to this point, our empirical discussions have only been focussed upon the missing slots (including inanimate noun phrases) in Japanese texts and their equivalent Agentive expressions in the corresponding English texts in the parallel corpora, yielding the clear-cut statistic data as illustrated in Tables 1 and 2. The figures in the tables clearly demonstrate the major contrast between the obfuscation of agency in Japanese in favour of impersonal construction of propositions *vs.* the accentuation of the agency concept in English which underlies the prevalence of the 'actor-action' pattern of clause formation. It must be borne in mind, however, that in addition to the opposition between English Agents and inanimate 'nothingness' in Japanese imbued with impersonality, there are also plenty of cases where English Agents correspond to Japanese noun phrases which are animate/human but not Agentive. What follows is one such instance which has been observed in the parallel corpora but has not been included in the numerical analysis in Tables 1 and 2:

(40) a. *Shikamo* <u>*senmonka*</u> <u>*ni-yoreba*</u>,   *Toresu no   jiken wa   hyōzan*
         Besides   expert   to-according, Torres GEN case   TOP iceberg

> *no   ikkaku   ni-sugi-nai.*
> GEN   one:corner   no:more:than-COP:NEG.
>
> (Text 4: Newsweek (Japanese edition), 31 August 1994)
>
> b.   And, if Torres and his associates could obtain ..., <u>authorities</u> say, it was
>   probable that others could, too.   (Text 4: *Newsweek*, 29 August 1994)

In (40a), the Japanese expression *senmonka* ('expert(s)'), which is to be classified as [+ animate], appears in a 'satellite' position inside a postpositional phrase, whilst its English counterpart in (40b), *authorities,* is clearly an Agent in a main clause in this piece of text. If such cases as above were to be taken into account, the Agentive oriented nature of English and the non-Agentive oriented nature of Japanese would be demonstrated even more strikingly.

A general conclusion drawn from the case study in this chapter is that, in Japanese, the agent (or the potential Agent) of an action often dissolves in some measure into nothingness, whereas, the tendency to express who/what performs an action prevails in English (Yamamoto 1999:174). On the one hand, Japanese is biassed towards impersonality, preferring an 'event-form' of clause construction, where the existence and actions of humans and animates tend to be 'submerged' in the 'whole course of an event' (Ikegami 1981, 1982 and 1991; Andō 1986; Yamamoto 1999). On the other hand, the favourite clause type in English is an 'actor-action form' which tends to highlight human/animate entities as 'Agents' (Bloomfield 1933; Dik 1989). Philosophically (and pragmatically) speaking, overtly expressing one's agency may have a face threatening effect, since, every so often, attribution of agency means accusation or assignment of responsibility (Davidson 1971; cf. also our arguments in Chapter 2). As has been argued in Section 2.4, English is sometimes quite sensitive to this potentially face threatening aspect of agency, but the statistical survey in the current chapter clearly demonstrated that Japanese is so much more sensitive to such an effect that it has developed the impersonal structure in constructing a proposition to obfuscate (or in many cases, completely 'efface') human agency, mitigating the sense of responsibility and accusation. Ikegami (1991) refers to this effacement of agency in Japanese as 'de-agentivisation', and it is clearly reflected in the phenomena of 'locationalisation' (Ikegami 1991) or 'positionalisation of persons' (Yamamoto 1992b), that have been mentioned earlier in the current chapter.

In the rest of this project, we will be going beyond the limit of the grammatical framework proposed by the Functional Grammarians (and their definitions of Agentivity and states of affairs). Obfuscating and impersonalising human agency and responsibility *vs.* articulating the personal aspect of agency: these two different manifestations of the agency concept in Japanese and English are suggestive of the different inner representations of outer reality and their intimate interconnection with linguistic structures. The following chapter will start with these opposite epistemic attitudes towards agency and will then attempt to elicit some clues to the characterisation of the concept of 'world-view' with reference to the so-called 'Sapir-Whorf hypothesis'.

Agency, impersonality and world-view

With reference to linguistic and socio-cultural relativity

… a paradox, namely that reality, as we know it, is exclusively composed of 'fancies'.

(Albert Einstein)[1]

4.1 Overview

Language and the inner representation of outer reality are so intimately interconncected, that, when talking about the concept of 'world-view', we cannot help getting into a 'chicken-and-egg dilemma' about which influences which (Fowler 1977:17). The linguistic manifestations of the agency concept in Japanese and English, which have been closely observed in the preceding chapter, seem to provide one good example that illustrates such a relationship between 'language and the inner representation of outer reality'. However, of course, it must be borne in mind that what human beings refer to as 'reality' itself can be the product of our subjective observation of the outside world; this is probably why Albert Einstein remarked that reality "is exclusively composed of 'fancies'", as in the above quotation.

In the current chapter, we will go beyond the limitation of the grammatical framework of agency proposed by the Functional Grammarians and will embark upon the further interpretation of the opposition between the obfuscation and the articulation of human agency. Investigating what the 'inner representations' of agency in the Japanese and English languages (and the different cultural values behind the surface linguistic phenomena) are will be our central concern here, which will develop into a wider characterisation of 'mind-style' or 'world-view', and it naturally follows, then, that we will have recourse to the 'relativistic' view on the interrelationship between language, thought and culture, not in pursuit of a deterministic idea on one's mother tongue dominating one's thought and behaviour, but in an attempt to shed some light upon what Fowler calls the 'chicken-and-egg dilemma'.

The following section will re-examine the propensity of the Japanese language for impersonalising human agency, as compared with the saliently foregrounded agency concept in English. Along with the cases which have already been observed within a particular grammatical framework in Chapter 3, those cases illustrating the less obvious manifestations of agency, that cannot be characterised within the Functional Grammarians' view on the semantic role of 'Agent', will also be taken into account, in search for the pragmatic and socio-cultural motives facilitating the particular patterns of encoding agency.

Then, the relationship between the concept of 'mind-style' or 'world-view' and the linguistic manifestations of agency (and impersonality) reflected in Japanese and English will further be elucidated in the light of 'linguistic relativity'. A brief remark on the historical background of 'Sapir-Whorf hypothesis' has already been given in Chapter 1; our task in Section 4.3 will be to make a closer sketch of what Whorf termed as the 'linguistic relativity principle',[2] which has been revisited in the recent intellectual climate particularly since the 1990s.

Finally, in Section 4.4, we will bring the theoretical discussions on linguistic (and socio-cultural) relativity into practice, at least partially, applying them to our current interest in the agency and impersonality concepts, with supplementary socio-cultural facts that throw some light upon the impersonal treatment of human agency in Japanese.

4.2 Loss of agency or expression of 'impersonality'

In the preceding chapter, I argued that the 'impersonal' nature of coding or not coding agency in Japanese ranges from the complete effacement of potential agents in constructing a clause to the use of alternative inanimate expressions or animate non-agentive noun phrases. Complete effacement of agents can be achieved by means of ellipsis in the majority of cases and sometimes through entirely impersonal constructions of sentences, which have quite a different status in current theoretical and descriptive studies from that of passive (Blevins 2003: 1).

4.2.1 Complete effacement of agents

What is the cognitive implication of the complete effacement of (potential) agents in describing a certain non-linguistic event? In answering this question at least partially, we can resort to the notion of 'frames of reference' in a more or less metaphorical way.

Originally, 'frame of reference' is a crucial concept to the study of human spatial cognition, and this idea is 'as old as the hills', dating back to, again, Aristotle's discussion on a boat moored in a flowing river (Levinson 2003: 6–7, 24–25). The long-disputed puzzle about this episode is that the boat in question can be interpreted as both moving and stationary, depending on the viewer's frame of reference. If we take the water in the river as 'frame of reference' (or reference point), it is perfectly logical to assume that the location of the boat is constantly changing, since the fluid in which it is moored is. However, we have to admit that this is quite counter-intuitive, and so Aristotle argued that the bank of the river must be adopted as a more proper frame of reference, since it is the nearest immobile surface (Levinson 2003:7).

In terms of the notion of 'frame of reference' in an original sense, the river bank in the above argument is to be labelled as 'landmark' or 'ground', and the boat moored in the river can be referred to as what has been termed as 'figure'. Following Talmy (1983), the notion of 'figure' can be defined as the cognitively salient object that is located and 'ground' the object with respect to which the 'figure' is located (cf. Bickel 1997:47). The following examples from English and the Mayan language Tzeltal (from Levinson 1996) clearly illustrate how these spatial subconcepts of frames of reference function effectively in explaining the construction of a clause:

(1)   The cat   is on the mat.
      (figure) (ground   )

(Levinson 1996:183)

(2)   *Pachal*   *ta mexa boch.*
      Sitting-bowl-like at table gourd.
      (ground   ) (figure)
      'The gourd is on the table'.   (Levinson 1996:184)

The English clause in (1), *The cat is on the mat*, states that the cognitively salient entity *the cat* can be found in a search-domain relative to the relatum or the 'ground'. In the Tzeltal clause in (2), the main object or the 'figure', *boch*, a type of bowl-shaped gourd, is specified by the predicate adjective *pachal*, which describes the upright location of a vessel-like object whose greatest diameter is not greater than its mouth (Levinson 1996:184).

When we apply the distinction between 'figure' and 'ground' to the Japanese clause construction, a sentence with an elliptical agent, such as (3) below, is to be interpreted as having no 'figure', but consists only of 'ground':

(3)   Ø   *Kyōto ni shibaraku   i-masu.*
      (I:NOM) Kyoto in for:a:while (will:)stay.
            (ground   )
      '(I) (will) stay in Kyoto for a while'.

A more complex exemplar of this kind was observed in Chapter 3 and is now repeated in (4a) below:

(4) a. "Ø   *Sutanbūru ni wa, sūjisu   go-tōryū   no*
          "(You:TOP) Stamboul   in TOP, few:days HON-sojourn LK
          go-yotei   de-gozaimasu ka?"
          HON-schedule COP-HON   QU?"

                                  (Text 2: Japanese translation of the below)

     b. "And <u>you</u> intend to remain there [in Stamboul] a few days, I think?"
                                  (Text 2: Agatha Christie, *Murder on the Orient Express*)

The statistical survey in Section 3.3 proved that ellipsis is the most predominant means of person reference in Japanese, but that it is by no means the case in English, and I argued that the use of ellipsis in place of human Agents 'impersonalises' the entire clause a great deal. In fact, it was found that, in the parallel Japanese-English corpora, as many as 80 instances amongst the total of 152 cases of Japanese non-Agents corresponding to English Agents are caused by ellipsis (see Table 1 in Chapter 3). In Example (4), which is also extracted from the parallel corpus, the equivalent of an English Agentive noun phrase *you* is a Japanese elliptical site, which does not originally consist of a part of an 'actor-action' form of clause construction. In terms of the concept of 'frame of reference', whereas the main clause in (4b) has *you* as its figure and the remaining verb phrase, *intend to remain there a few days*, as its ground, the Japanese translational clause in (4a) has no figure, but consists only of its ground.

The English gloss of the translational Japanese clause in (4a) goes something like: "(As for you), in Stamboul (Istanbul), is a few day's stay the (your) schedule?" It is obvious that the non-existence of a cognitively salient human entity contributes a great deal to the impersonal tone of the sentence in question. Under a different guise, in (4a), the 'figure' which is to be 'located' in Stamboul (Istanbul) for a couple of days does not exist or is hidden/covered under the veil of ellipsis as if it is a part of the 'ground'.

In observing the examples in (3) and (4), it can be interpreted that the omission of actors (or Agents in Simon Dik's terms) means the omission of figures at the same time. For more instances of this sort extracted from the parallel corpora, see examples (28)–(31) back in Chapter 3. However, as far as this particular case in Example (4a) is concerned, this is not the whole picture. As I argued in Section 3.3, because of the absence of the potential human agent, the inherent nature of the entire 'event' itself is expressed in an impersonal way. In other words, the loss of a saliently personal 'figure' results in the impersonalisation of the relevant 'ground'. In the terminology of Functional Grammar *a la* Simon Dik (1989), the relevant event described in (4a) is deprived of 'dynamicity' and the human 'control' over it; the state of affairs involved in this clause is not that of 'Action' but that of 'State'. Whilst the English original highlights the intentionality of the Agent, the Japanese translation expresses the entire State as if it is an established fact without regard to the addressee's spontaneous intentionality (Yamamoto 1999: 167), submerging the protagonist in the 'ground'.

Lee (1996: 28) argues after Whorf (1956) that in either the 'external' or 'egoic' (internal) fields of experience, isolates are experienced as either 'figure' or 'ground' abstracted from the ongoing flux of perceptual stimulation. It is interesting to note that Whorf himself (1956: 162–163) suggests a relationship of certain measure between the opposition of 'actor' and 'action' and that of 'figure' and 'ground' as the means of 'segmenting' certain situation or experience. He further maintains that the latter distinction is more cognitively 'universal' (i.e. more widely acceptable to 'all observers', including the native speakers of a wide range of non-Indo-European languages) than the former, which he regards as a product of typically Indo-European way of dissecting the world, along with such distinction as that between 'subject' and 'predicate'.

As our discussions in Chapter 3 (and the present chapter, too) clearly demonstrate, the contrastive notions of 'actor' and 'action' can be effectively applied to (at least) a language like Japanese, which is obviously outside the Indo-European linguistic stock; however, Whorf's above argument regarding the distinction between 'figure' and 'ground' and the dichotomies such as subject-predicate and actor-action is still of considerable interest. Why then is the absence of a 'figure' more basic (or more widely applicable) kind of 'nothingness' than that of an actor?

The basic concepts of figure and ground seem quite widely applicable to the description of clauses which are not focussed on spatial relationship of objects; for example, Ikegami's (1982 and 1991) 'hypothesis' regarding the two extreme tendencies of highlighting and obfuscating human, agentive entities involved in certain actions and events can be reinterpreted from a fresher point of view here. Ikegami's argument which we examined in detail in the previous chapter was as follows:

(5)　There is a contrast between (1) a language which focuses on 'the human being (especially, one acting as agent)' and tends to give linguistic prominence to the notion [of agency] and (2) a language which tends to suppress the notion of 'the human being (especially, one acting as agent)', even if such a being is involved in the event.　　　　　　　　　　　　　　　(Ikegami 1991: 290)

If the domain of the contrastive notions of 'figure' and 'ground' is to be enhanced metaphorically to the non-spatial realm of human experience, it is the human element in Ikegami's hypothesis that corresponds to the concept of 'figure', and the 'event' concept corresponds to that of 'ground'. The loss of an actor in the actor-action form of clause construction certainly impersonalises the entire clause. However, it is the absence of 'figure' which keeps the entire event or situation in question in the background: in this sense, it can be argued, following Whorf, that the lack of 'figure' in terms of the concept of frame of reference represents a more significant nothingness (or impersonality) than that of an agent, although the absence of these two fundamental conceptual elements may coincide with each other in the majority of the cases, as we have observed in the examples above.

It has been observed from Table 1 in Chapter 3 that English Agentive items have no equivalent noun phrases whatsoever in the corresponding Japanese texts in 64 cases out of the total of 152 cases of English Agents corresponding to Japanese non-Agentive NPs in the parallel corpora. As I have argued in the preceding chapter, the most predominant reason for this structural loss of Japanese Agentive expressions seems to be that Japanese tends not to dissect a proposition into an 'actor' and an 'action' in Bloomfield's (1933) terms, as many European languages including English do (Yamamoto 1999).

Another instance, which has also been observed in Chapter 3, can be re-examined in terms of metaphorically enhanced notions of 'figure' and 'ground'. In what follows, the Japanese sentence lacks both an 'Agent' and a 'figure', but, unlike the cases we have seen so far in (3) and (4), the loss is not caused by ellipsis but by originally impersonal packaging of information. The Agent in the English translational text (in (6b)), *Kenzo*, has no corresponding NP (not even an elliptical site) in the Japanese original; in other words, neither an Agent nor a 'figure' are incorporated into (6a) in the first place.

(6)   a.   *"Fufu".*
           (ground)
                              (Text 1: Yukio Mishima, *Hyaku-man Yen Sembei*)

      b.   Kenzo   laughed.
           (figure) (ground)
                              (Text 1: English translation of the above)

The above set of examples illustrates a case where an English clause containing an Agentive entity does not have an equivalent clause in a corresponding piece of Japanese text, which is structurally fully-fledged. In the original Japanese expression in (6a), a simple onomatopoeic word, *fufu*, tells the readers what they need to know to understand the situation; obviously, this form does not consist of an 'actor' and 'action'. Further, being an onomatopoeia, it is inevitably impersonal and functions like 'background music' or 'sound effects' of some sort in the novel. However, '*fufu*' also conveys the same amount of information as that carried by an English 'actor-action' sentence in (6b) with its Agent, *Kenzo*, which (who) is also the 'figure' in this clause, being a salient protagonist. Whilst the English clause in (6b) has both 'figure' and 'ground', the equivalent Japanese expression consists only of 'ground' which does not represent any 'action'. This case can be classified as an ultimate demonstration of impersonality in the Japanese language, which still corresponds to a highly personal and agentive English sentence.

Other instances of impersonal constructions, which can be found commonly in the Japanese language, are not concerned with the presence and absence of 'figures' as distinct from 'ground'. Such cases also illustrate the clear opposition between saliently articulated agency in English and entirely effaced agency in Japanese. Study again the following instances taken from *Newsweek* and Yukio Mishima's *Hyaku-man Yen Sembei*, which are repeated below in (7) and (8) respectively. The potentially Agentive elements in the Japanese texts are perfectly 'hidden' without undergoing ellipsis and can only be inferred from the context.

(7) a.   <u>Doitsu de-wa</u>   *5-gatsu irai,*   *heiki*   *ni tenyō dekiru*
           <u>Germany in-</u>TOP May   since,   weapon   to divert can
           shōryō   *no purutoniumu ya   uran   ga   hokani*
           small:amount LK plutonium   and uranium NOM additionally
           3-kai   *mo ōshū-sare-teiru.*
           three-times   seize-PASS-PERF.
                              (Text 4: *Newsweek* (Japanese edition), 31 August 1994)
     b.   Since May, <u>German officials</u> have made three other seizures of tiny amounts of weapons-grade plutonium and uranium.
                              (Text 4: *Newsweek*, 29 August 1994)

Both (7a) and (7b) have 'figures' and 'grounds' in a metaphorical sense. On the one hand, the figure in the English original is *German officials*, referring to the Agent of the action of confiscation. The Japanese clause in (7a), on the other hand, has the plutonium and uranium good enough to be used for weapons as its figure; they are the commodities that were confiscated by the 'hidden' agents. This contrast means that the focal points in the Japanese and English texts are quite different, and it can be argued that the difference derives from the two distinctive mind-styles at work in constructing propositions. The original English clause dissects the event in question into the actor or the Agent, 'German officials', and what they did, i.e. confiscating the dangerous, radioactive commodity. The corresponding Japanese translational clause in (7a), however, expresses the same event in the form of a 'Process' (but not an 'Action') in Simon Dik's terms with *no* reference at all to the agency of the heroic German officials. Simply, a sensational event – i.e. the confiscation of plutonium and uranium – took place somewhere *in Germany* for three times, and that is enough.

Example (8) below also demonstrates the clear opposition between the clause construction of the 'event pattern' and that of the 'actor-action pattern' in Japanese and English. This passage is a critical account of a funfair where organisers plan so that masses of folk spend a lot of money: potentially, there can be two different kinds of agency at work – that of those making money and that of those wasting it.

(8) a.   "...*Kōyū tokoro wa,   hitotsu hitotsu wa   yasui   yō   demo,*
"...Such place TOP, one   one   TOP cheap seem though,
kekkyoku omoigake-nai o-kane o   tsuka-waseru   yō-ni
eventually unexpected   money ACC spend-cause:PART as
deki-teru   n-da-mono".
made-PART COP".

(Text 1: Yukio Mishima, *Hyaku-man Yen Sembei*)

b.   "... Everything seems so cheap, but it's all arranged so that [you spend
more money than you intend to]".

(Text 1: English translation of the above)

The original Japanese text and its English translation reflect the completely different interpretations of the scene of a funfair and present an interesting contrast
between the prototypical mind-styles manifested in the two languages. In (8a),
no agency and intentionality of both parties – the enterprisers and consumers –
is encoded; as we have observed in the preceding chapter, the speaker constructs
her argument in a perfectly impersonal manner: a funfair is arranged in such and
such a way. In the terminology of Functional Grammarians, the 'state of affairs'
expressed in this sentence is that of a 'Situation' (more precisely, a State, which is
[– control]) but not that of an 'Action' with an 'actor' and his/her 'action'.

Conversely, the English translational text in (8b) clearly expresses the agency
of those who spend their money in a parenthetical clause, whose 'figure' is *you*,
who could be either Kenzo, the speaker's husband and the main character of this
novel, or – more likely – countless folk like him who may waste money for something silly. In English, by the use of generic personal pronouns, the 'actor-action'
pattern of clause construction can be maintained; we shall discuss this point in
more detail later in Section 4.4. The figure of the main clause in the Japanese original text is the noun phrase, *kōyū tokoro* ('such a place', i.e. a funfair), and the
rest of the clause (or the 'ground') describes the characteristics of such a place.
The foci of the Japanese original text and its corresponding English translation
are on a place and on human agents respectively; this is a significant factor which
characterises the typically Japanese and English 'mind-styles', and the following
subsection will provide many more convincing examples. However, despite the
above difference, what is commonly shared by the Japanese and English texts in
(8) is that the state of affairs in the main clauses is that of a 'State', which describes
how a funfair is arranged and does not reveal the hidden agency and intentionality
of the organisers.

As we have seen in Section 2.4, agency can be hidden and covered up in any
language. What reveals much about the 'mind-styles' or 'world-views' of the language users is the extent to which it is obfuscated and the manner in which it is
typically submerged in the whole course of an event.

4.2.2 Non-complete effacement/obfuscation

The expression of the agency concept is a matter of gradience that ranges from the complete 'effacement' of potentially agentive entities to privileging agents with the most salient grammatical position in a sentence. The 'impersonal' nature of encoding agency in Japanese manifests itself in the form of either the complete loss of potentially agentive elements (of which instances have been discussed in the last subsection) or the non-complete effacement or obfuscation of human/animate entities being referred to by means of animate but non-agentive noun phrases or, in some cases, alternative inanimate expressions. Conversely, the 'agentive' nature of English person reference, in the majority of cases, tends to grant potential agents the grammatically salient status as sentential subjects. It naturally follows then that, as the findings of the investigation into the parallel Japanese/English corpora show, an English Agentive noun phrase may quite frequently correspond to a Japanese non-Agentive, inanimate expression.

In the current subsection, we will observe the cases of the non-complete effacement/obfuscation of agents in Japanese corpus data and the strikingly different manifestations (and interpretations) of the same (potentially) agentive entities in the corresponding English texts. The examples here will illustrate that the loss of agentive entities does not always coincide with the absence of 'figures', which is, according to Whorf, cognitively more fundamental than that of 'actors'. The scope of our discussion here will be broader than that of the preceding chapter – those cases which do not come under the Functional Grammarians' framework of semantic roles will also be taken into account.

Our particular foci will be upon the phenomena of 'de-agentivisation' including (1) 'locationalisation' (cf. Ikegami 1991) or 'positionalisation' of persons (cf. Yamamoto 1992b) as the manifestation of the 'impersonality' concept in Japanese and (2) the opposition between individualistic agency, which is prevalent in the English way of person reference, and group agency or 'collective' agency, which often conceals the involvement of individuals in certain events in Japanese and deprives certain actions of a personal (and individual) sense of responsibility as actors.[3] The two aspects of 'impersonality' mentioned above – that is, 'locationalisation' or 'positionalisation' of persons and the notion of 'group' or 'collective' agency – are not totally autonomous, but are closely intertwined with each other, and, as our examples will demonstrate, institutionalised forms of agency can often be associated with a metaphorical sense of positionalisation of persons. Observing the gulf between the 'inner representations' of agency in these two languages will pave the way to our later discussions on linguistic and socio-cultural relativity.

First of all, a very straightforward example of 'locationalisation' or 'positionalisation of persons' can be found in what follows, where a place name can stand

for an individual human being or a group of human beings (Yamamoto 1999:21).
If one has a relative who lives in the city of Nagoya, he/she may say something like:

(9)   *Nagoya   wa   kono   ken   ni-wa   hantai   rashii.*
      Nagoya   TOP   this   issue   about   against   it:seem.
      'Nagoya seems to be against this issue'.

Japanese exhibits general liability to the metonymic phenomena concerning geographic entities; it is not uncommon that individual human beings can be referred to by the name of a place where they live as a *part* of their identity. The pragmatic implication of such uses of terms designating places – which are literally inanimate – as a means of person reference is that they mitigate the sense of the referents' personal agency and responsibility, the entire clause sounding more like a static 'process' than a dynamic 'action'. In (9), the subject *Nagoya* may possibly be interpreted as a Force on the level of lexical semantics, but, at least on a pragmatic level, it is to be regarded as an Agent with more or less a limited sense of responsibility and dynamicity.

It must be borne in mind, however, that this phenomenon is not unique to Japanese. It is generally recognised that, in English, too, a place name may be used to metonymically designate human entities (Lakoff 1987:77), as the following examples illustrate:

(10) a.   *Wall street* is in a panic.   (Lakoff 1987:77)
      b.   BMW's £800m take over means that, for the first time in 112 years, *Britain* no longer boasts a British-owned volume car maker.
                                                        (*The Independent*, 1 February 1994)
      c.   *Greece* was plunged into immediate mourning after hearing her [Melina Mercouri's] death in a news flash.   (*The Times*, 7 March 1994)

However, without doubt, the frequency with which this linguistic phenomenon of 'locationalisation' occurs is much greater in Japanese than in English.

Examples (11) and (14) below clearly illustrate the manifestations of the impersonality concept in Japanese in terms of the 'locationalisation' or 'positionalisation' of human agents. As I have demonstrated in Table 1 in Chapter 3, amongst the total of 152 cases of English Agents corresponding to Japanese non-Agentive NPs in the parallel corpora, 8 cases have been found where English Agentive noun phrases have inanimate (and naturally non-Agentive) expressions as their counterparts, which are not elliptical, but encoded verbally. Consider again the following example extracted from a *Newsweek* article on the Russian nuclear threat, where both Japanese and English clauses have 'figures':[4]

(11) a. *Kore ni taishite* <u>*Roshia-gawa*</u> *wa   senshū   hajime,   kengi*
          This to against <u>Russian-side</u> NOM last:week beginning, suspicion
          o   tsuyoku   hitei.
          ACC strongly deny.
                              (Text 4: *Newsweek* (Japanese edition), 31 August 1994)
       b. Early last week the Russians hotly denied that the rogue plutonium was
           theirs.   (Text 4: *Newsweek*, 29 August 1994)

In reading (11b), the original English sentence, one could be most likely to imagine
some angry Russian officials 'hotly' arguing against what they see as Western bias.
The underlined noun phrase, *the Russians*, which is the subject of the main clause,
is clearly a grammatical Agent in Dik's terms and imbued with strong personality
and responsibility for what they insist.

In the Japanese translational text in (11a), however, the expression *Roshia-
gawa* ('Russian side') does not refer to individual human beings, but suggests a certain political 'position' of the country, and, as argued earlier, it is a typical manifestation of 'positionalisation (or locationalisation) of persons' (cf. Yamamoto 1992b;
Ikegami 1991). The suffix '-*gawa*' meaning 'side' is used when the writer/speaker
makes contrast between more than two contradictory positions or opinions.
Grammatically speaking, the noun phrase *Roshia-gawa* ('Russian side') is a 'Force',
since it is inanimate as an entity in itself, and it is highly unlikely that the Japanese
subscribers to *Newsweek* would visualise angry, individual Russians, when they en-
counter the text in (11a). An important implication (and effect) of this is that an
impersonal expression with less agency naturally encodes less responsibility.

These completely different impressions that the English original and Japanese
translational texts leave on readers' minds can be ascribed to the strikingly different 'inner representations of agency' in these languages and the distinctive 'mind-
styles' or 'world-views' behind the logic through which these pieces of text are
formed. With no doubt, the expression and suppression of agency, animacy and
responsibility must be regarded as some of the most fundamental aspects of highly
significant linguistic determiners of mind-styles/world-views in the two languages
in question (cf. Fowler 1977: 106).

Alongside the concept of agency itself, Japanese person referential expressions
tend to suppress the 'individuation' concept, which we considered as one of the
interacting parameters of 'animacy' (see Section 2.5). The noun *Roshia* ('Russia')
in *Roshia-gawa* ('Russian side') is obviously the name of a nation, which is a 'local community' or a 'geographical entity', signifying a group of a vast number of
human beings; naturally, it is, in itself, an inanimate and thus non-agentive entity.
This means that when talking about a country, say, 'Russia', we are not focussing
on the responsibility and agency of individual Russians but treating them as a part
of a whole, collective mass.

Talking about the individual Russians as in the original English text in (11b) is completely a different matter. On the one hand, the Japanese way of paying attention to the inhuman agency of a country rather than that of its people further implies that the speaker/writer focusses upon a collective or group agency but not upon individual human agency; however, on the other hand, the English style of expressing the same event (or action) suggests that the speaker's/writer's attention is directed to the personal and individual aspect of human agency. Thus, the problem which Example (11) presents is not only that of positionalisation of persons but also that of the opposition between group agency and individual human agency.

As far as the expression of the 'individuation' concept is concerned, it has been statistically demonstrated that, whereas typically Japanese mind-style is apt to be focussed on countries, typically English mind-style tends to be more interested in individuated human entities living there (Yamamoto 1999:138–145). Indeed, Ikegami (1991) proposes another principle – or 'hypothesis' as he calls it – regarding the manifestation of the individuation concept in English and Japanese as in (12) on top of the one concerning agency, that we have examined above:

(12)   There is a contrast between (1) a language which, singling out an individuum, places the focus on it and (2) a language which focuses on the event as a whole, the individua involved in it being submerged in the whole.

(Ikegami 1991:290)

Evidently, Ikegami construes that English exhibits a strong tendency for the first mode of treating an 'individuum', and that Japanese for the second: English tends to overtly highlight the individuation concept, whilst Japanese tends to cover up its prominence under the veil of an 'event as a whole'.

Our corpus data also supports the above 'hypothesis'. In the journalistic texts within the parallel Japanese/English corpora (i.e. Texts 3 and 4), there are 23 cases (out of the total of 600), where English animate/individuated expressions correspond to Japanese inanimate/unindividuated expressions;[5] Examples (11), (14) and (16) are the specimens of such cases extracted from the journalistic Japanese/English corpus. In 5 cases out of 23, whilst the Japanese texts are concerned with countries, their corresponding English texts talk about their people. An extract from another *Newsweek* article in (13) does not contain any notable manifestation of agency, but illustrates the contrast between country *vs.* individual focus:

(13) a. *Kokusai   tero   no   shuryū   o   nashi-tei-ta*
          International terrorism GEN mainstream ACC form-ing-PAST
          Paresuchina minzoku undō   desura,   ima de-wa Isuraeru
          Palestinian   ethnic   movement NOM:even, now at-TOP Israel
          to-no wahei ni muka-tte   susun-deiru.
          with peace to head-PART advance-PROG.
                            (Text 4: *Newsweek* (Japanese edition), 31 August 1994)
      b. Even the mainstream Palestinian movement, so long a source of violence,
          has now turned toward peace with the Israelis.
                                          (Text 4: *Newsweek*, 29 August 1994)

As the underlines indicate, the Japanese noun phrase, *Isuraeru* ('Israel') in (13a),
which refers to a nation, corresponds to the English noun phrase, *the Israelis* in
(13b).

   In the extract (14) below, we can observe an even 'purer' instance of the
positionalisation of an individual human agent than the example in (11).

(14) a. *Karuban Kurain ni* "*Kenedī   jaketto*" *toyū na   no futatsu botan*
          Calvin Klein at   "Kennedy jacket" that name LK two   button
          no burezā ga   chanto aru.
          LK blazer NOM readily exist.
                             (Text 4: *Newsweek* (Japanese edition), 7 September 1994)
      b. Of course, every Jackie needs a Jack, so Calvin Klein's less-expensive
          CK menswear line includes a two-button blazer that he's dubbed "the
          Kennedy jacket".   (Text 4: *Newsweek*, 29 August 1994)

Nearly the same situation is encoded in two completely different fashions here.
As I have already argued in Chapter 3, in the Japanese translational text in (14a),
Calvin Klein (or *Karuban Kurain* in Japanese) is treated as a designer's studio *where*
'the Kennedy jacket' is produced, with the postposition *ni* (translated as 'at' in
the word-for-word translation) signifying a location. In the centre of this clause,
there is the famous 'Kennedy Jacket', which is its 'figure'. The 'locationalised' or
'positionalised' designer is impersonalised as a 'location' or a 'venue', where the
production of this particular commodity takes place, but this is not the end of the
story; Calvin Klein is also deprived of a privileged status as the 'figure' of a clause
and submerged as a part of its 'ground'.

   However, in the original English version of *Newsweek*, *Calvin Klein* is highlighted more saliently as an individual designer, who is the grammatical Agent of
the action of naming his blazer as 'the Kennedy jacket'. In (14b), the underline
shows that *he* referring to Calvin Klein himself is not only the Agent of the relative
clause modifying *a two-button blazer* but also the 'figure' of the same clause with
his 'Kennedy jacket' constituting a part of the 'ground'.

In this example, the human, potential agent is Calvin Klein, who is a public figure, and public figures can often be regarded as socio-cultural icons and therefore as possessing quite an impersonal mode of existence. This seems to be an extra factor which may have facilitated the impersonalisation or positionalisation of a human entity here, in addition to the fact that the name of this individual also means his world-famous brand. However, it is also noteworthy that, in Japanese, even a complete non-celebrity can naturally be impersonalised in the same way as someone super-famous. Consider the following example:

(15)　a.　*Jon　ni-wa　kodomo　ga　futari　iru.*
　　　　　　John　to-TOP　child(ren)　NOM　two:persons　exist.
　　　　　　'To John, two children exist'.
　　　　b.　John has two children.

The Japanese sentence in (15a) contains an instance of 'positionalisation of persons', which is outside the scope of the grammaticalisation of agency in Simon Dik's sense. '*Jon*' in (15a) is supposed to refer to an ordinary, everyday human being but undergoes exactly the same process of impersonalisation as Calvin Klein (or *Karuban Kurain*) in (14a), being encoded as a part of the 'ground' of the clause and treated as if it (or he) is a place where his two sons 'exist' (or belong to). In the corresponding English sentence, *John* is not an Agent but is given a salient position as a 'figure' and as a grammatical subject.

Like (15) above, the following passage does not illustrate any 'surface', grammatical manifestation of agency, but is also of considerable interest if we enhance our scope of the agency concept beyond Simon Dik's framework:

(16)　a.　*Murayama　seiken　　　wa　igai-ni　　　nagamochi-shi　sō*
　　　　　　Murayama　administration　TOP　unexpectedly　last:long-to:do　seem

　　　　　　da　toyū kansoku　　ga　Nagata-chō de　tsuyoma-tteiru.
　　　　　　AUX　that　observation　NOM　Nagata-Town in　become:strong-PROG.
　　　　　　　　　　　　　　　　　　(Text 3: *Asahi Shimbun*, 6 September 1994)
　　　　b.　A view has been gaining ground among Diet members that Murayama government is likely to stay for a longer period than was at first widely thought.
　　　　　　(Text 3: *Asahi Evening News* (English translation of the above), 6 September 1994)

The above text is an extract from an article which deals with a somewhat unstable-looking cabinet of a Social Democrat prime minister in the Japanese political world of the mid-1990s. The English translational text in (16b) contains a noun phrase, *Diet members*, which is in a 'satellite' position, and hence can never be classified as a grammatical Agent in the Functional Grammarians' terms. However, semantically speaking, it is these 'Diet members' who both animatedly and consciously ponder over the cabinet's future, and they may well be labelled as 'semantic agents'. This expression, therefore, refers to a set of fairly animated, individual human beings, and it is actually quite likely that the readers, who are knowledgeable enough about Japanese politics in the recent past, may be able to figure out *who* were amongst these 'Diet members'.

The Japanese original text in (16a), on the other hand, demonstrates how potential human agents can be encoded both as a faceless, unindividuated mass and as a mere 'place', where such a mass of people exists (Yamamoto 1999: 143). The underlined expression, *Nagata-chō* ('Nagata-Town'), is literally an area in the heart of Tokyo, which symbolically refers to the political world of Japan; the postposition *de*, that accompanies *Nagata-chō*, designates a location ('in' in the word-for-word translation). The current instance has much in common with Example (9) above, where a place name is metonymically employed to refer to individual and agentive human entities: *Nagoya wa kono ken ni-wa hantai rashii* ('Nagoya seems to be against this issue').

On the whole, the same situation is described in two strikingly different ways in (16a) and (16b). On the one hand, the Japanese text puts it as if a certain 'event' or 'process', i.e. a forecast of the near future of the current government, is taking place somewhere, that is, in Nagata-chō, the centre of the Japanese political world. But on the other hand, in the English translational text, the whole sentence is constructed so that individual politicians are actively 'doing something'.

What is behind these surface phenomena of 'positionalisation of persons' in Japanese, then? It is, without doubt, a prototypically Japanese way of viewing the world, which metaphorically expresses 'persons' in terms of 'positions' – primarily 'spatial' and secondarily 'social'. As we have seen so far, expressing human entities as 'positions' of some measure functions as a means of obfuscating (individual) human agency and responsibility, thus satisfying both conscious and unconscious drive for avoiding 'face threatening acts (FTAs)' (Yamamoto 1999: Chs. 1 and 3; see also Section 2.4 of this book). Later in the present chapter, we shall see the further conceptual implications of our findings as a part of a more general characteristic of person reference in this language as distinct from that of English. Before then, in the remainder of this section, two more important issues must be addressed: (1) metaphorical form of 'positionalisation of persons' with a particular focus on 'social' roles and (2) opposition between group agency and individual agency.

The most notable 'metaphorical' form of positionalisation of persons is the use of social deictic terms (in an everyday, pretheoretical sense) as a means of person reference, the association between physical, spatial positions and the description of one's social positions, statuses or roles being quite a straightforward one. Japanese speakers and writers tend to employ common noun phrases repeatedly to refer to the same individuals, and these terms designate the roles/functions of the referents and their relations to other individuals (Yamamoto 1999: 134). The reason why Japanese native speakers feel more comfortable with using common noun phrases, which denote the referents' social standings of some measure, rather than personal pronouns, which do not, depends heavily upon Japanese socio-cultural values, which will be explored in Section 4.4 in the light of the linguistic relativity hypothesis. Along with the impersonalisation effects that such socially-oriented common noun phrases have, the opposite, personalisation effects brought forth by the use of personal pronouns will also be considered in Section 4.4.

As many have argued, for the Japanese, 'roles' are particular behavioural patterns which an individual is expected to acquire or follow in a certain socio-cultural context (see, for instance, Minoura 1991: 51). This can be regarded as one form of 'unindividuation' or 'impersonalisation' of human entities and is found clearly and pervasively in the use of referential expressions in Japanese (Yamamoto 1999: 134). The results of the case studies of Japanese/English parallel corpora (using Texts 1 to 6) clearly support the argument that, on the one hand, the Japanese language tends to express human beings as social roles, positions, statuses, etc. by means of common noun phrases, and that, on the other hand, English is prone to encode a strong sense of individuation and animacy when referring to human entities by the overwhelming use of personal (and possessive) pronouns (Yamamoto 1999: 135). In a large number of cases, Japanese common noun phrases are found to have pronominal equivalents in the corresponding English texts.

As I have demonstrated earlier in Yamamoto (1999: 135), out of 441 common noun phrases in the Japanese texts (Texts 1 to 6), 34 noun phrases (7.71% of the total number of common noun phrases) correspond to English personal and possessive pronouns. Conversely, there is only *one* English common noun phrase designating a social role of a human entity (0.22%), out of the total of 455, whose Japanese equivalent is a personal pronoun. Some of the cases where Japanese common noun phrases designating social roles correspond to English personal pronouns are presented in (17), (18) and (19) below.

(17) a. *Kenzō wa   sakkino   sora-tobu enban o,   gangu uriba*
          Kenzo NOM above:mentioned sky-flying saucer ACC, toy   counter
          no mae o   tō-tte   uriko   ni kaeshi-ta   ga,
          LK front ACC go:through-ing salesgirl to return-PAST but,
          uketoru   uriko   wa fukigen-ni yoko o   mui-ta   mama te
          receive:ing salesgirl NOM grumpily side ACC turn-ing still   hand
          o   dashi-ta.
          ACC stick:out-PAST.

                                    (Text 1: Yukio Mishima, *Hyaku-man Yen Sembei*)

      b. Kenzo brought the flying saucer back to the toy counter. The salesgirl, out
          of sorts, looked away as she reached to take it.

                              (Text 1: English translation of the above by Edward Seidensticker)

In (17a), the Japanese original text, 'the salesgirl' is referred to in terms of her social role/position as an *uriko* (literally meaning 'salesgirl') each time this same individual is mentioned, but in the English translational text in (17b), the same human entity is referred to as *she* by means of a personal pronoun after the first mention.

In the extract (18) below, Mr Tomiichi Murayama, a former Prime Minister of Japan, is first introduced with his full name and full title in both Japanese and English articles – *Murayama Tomiichi shushō* or Prime Minister Tomiichi Murayama.

(18) a. *Murayama Tomiichi <u>shushō</u>*   *ga   Azia yon-ka-koku   no*
         Murayama Tomiichi <u>prime:minister</u> NOM Asia four-countries LK
         Ø   tabi o   oe-ta.
         (his) trip ACC finish-PAST.
         <u>Shushō</u>   wa   kono rekihō de, Ø   nerai-to-shi-ta Azia
         <u>Prime:minister</u> NOM this visit by, (he) aim-PART   Asia
         jūshi   no shisei   o,   mazu wa
         attach:ing:importance LK attitude ACC, in:the:first:place
         shime-se-ta   no-de-wa-nai-ka.
         show-can-PAST AUX.
                                          (Text 3: *Asahi Shimbun*, 31 August 1994)
      b. <u>Prime Minister</u> Tomiichi Murayama has completed his visit to four coun-
         tries in Asia. <u>He</u> may be said to have shown to Asian leaders how much
         importance Japan attaches to Asian countries, as <u>he</u> has intended, during
         <u>his</u> trip.   (Text 3: *Asahi Evening News*, 31 August 1994)

In (18a), Murayama is referred to as *shushō* ('Prime Minister') in terms of his so-cial position/role for the second time. Conversely, its corresponding form in the English translational text, (18b), is *he*, and once personal and possessive pronouns are introduced (*he* and *his* in this case), they are continuously used, without en-coding the social standing of the referent, unless potential ambiguity arises (cf. Yamamoto 1999:136).

The extract in (19) from a journal in computer science illustrates an even clearer case of encoding impersonality by a common noun phrase, which is a large-scale linguistic phenomenon in Japanese, but not in English:

(19) a. *<u>Hissha-ra</u> wa,   shizen gengo   o   mochi-ita taiwa   ni-yotte*
         <u>Authors</u>   NOM, natural language ACC use-ing   dialogue by
         yūzā no   keisanki riyō o   shien-suru taiwa-gata   herupu
         user GEN computer use ACC help-ing   dialogue-type help
         shisutemu no kōchiku   o   okonat-teiru.
         system   LK construction ACC carry:out-PROG.

(Text 5: *The Transactions of the Institute of Electronics, Information and Communication Engineers*)

b. <u>We</u> are developing a computer-based consultant system that helps novice computer users by allowing spoken dialogues.

(Text 5: *Systems and Computers in Japan* (English translation of the above))

The Japanese expression *hissha-ra* ('authors') in (19a) not only encodes the referents' social role/position, but gives the entire text a somewhat impersonal tone (cf. Yamamoto 1999: Chs. 3 and 4). The corresponding form in the English translation, *we*, conveys a more personal and more agentive touch.

The pervasive use of social roles/positions in making person reference in the Japanese language coupled with rarely used personal 'pronouns' will be analysed from a cognitive and socio-cultural perspective in Section 4.4 in association with the theoretical complex of linguistic relativity, which basically suggests the closely-knit co-relationship between 'language', 'thought' and 'culture'.

The final element to be examined in this section is group (or collective/institutionalised) agency as a form of 'impersonalisation' or 'impersonality' in making person reference, with which the concept of individuation intervenes. As mentioned earlier, 'group agency' is intimately intertwined with 'positionalisation' or 'locationalisation' of persons. Recall the example (11) again where the English expression *the Russians* makes a clear contrast to the corresponding Japanese (translational) expression *Roshia-gawa*, meaning 'the Russian side', as a typical instance of the manifestation of group/collective agency in the Japanese language.

(11) a. *Kore ni taishite <u>Roshia-gawa</u> wa   senshū   hajime,   kengi*
          This to   against   <u>Russian-side</u> NOM last:week beginning, suspicion
          o   tsuyoku hitei.
          ACC strongly deny.
          (Text 4: *Newsweek* (Japanese edition), 31 August 1994)
      b. Early last week <u>the Russians</u> hotly denied that the rogue plutonium was theirs.
          (Text 4: *Newsweek*, 29 August 1994)

The inclination of Japanese towards group/collective agency rather than individual human agency is clearly reflected in the piece of statistical data given earlier in this section. In the journalistic texts within the parallel Japanese/English corpora (i.e. Texts 3 and 4), there are 23 cases (out of the total 600), where English animate/individuated expressions correspond to Japanese collective (inanimate and unindividuated) expressions. Conversely, there are 7 cases where Japanese animate/individuated noun phrases correspond to English collective expressions.

Two more typical examples of the opposition between Japanese group/collective agency and English individualistic agency are found in (20) and (21) below:

(20) a. [*Kurinton seiken*   *ga*   *mizukara*   *seoikon-da*]   *seiji*
           [Clinton administration NOM voluntarily shoulder-PART] political
           kadai
           problem
                                              (Text 3: *Asahi Shimbun*, 20 September 1994)

      b. a political problem [that <u>President Clinton himself</u> stepped forward to
           tackle in the first place]
           (Text 3: *Asahi Evening News* (the English translation of the above), 20
           September 1994)

In (20a) and (20b), an interesting contrast is found in the relative clauses marked with square brackets, which modify the noun phrases *seiji kadai* or *a political problem*. Syntactically speaking, the Japanese clause encapsulates the 'Process' as if the decision has been made collectively and hence impersonally, employing an inanimate 'Force', *Kurinton seiken* ('Clinton administration'). Semantically and pragmatically speaking, however, the Japanese expression *Kurinton seiken* ('Clinton administration') refers to an inanimate (or, to a certain extent, abstract) group agent *which* makes a collective decision and acts collectively. On the other hand, its English counterpart intensifies the individualistic agency and responsibility of Bill Clinton as an individual 'Agent', with the reflexive pronoun *himself* accompanying the Agentive noun phrase *President Clinton*.

The case in Extract (21) is completely outside the grammatical framework of agency by Simon Dik:

(21) a. *Saiban no   shōten wa,* Ø <u>*Keisatsu-chō*</u> *no   shiji   nado ni*
           Case   GEN focus TOP (it) <u>Police-Agency</u> GEN order etc.   on
           motozuku soshikitekina tōchō   to mitome-rareru ka-dōka, ni
           base:PART institutional bugging as recognise-PASS whether, on
           a-tta.
           be-PAST.
                                              (Text 3: *Asahi Shimbun*, 7 September 1994)

      b. The public's attention in the case was focused on whether the bugging
           would be recognized by the court as an institutional act ordered by <u>the
           officers on a high echelon</u>, such as the National Police Agency.
           (Text 3: *Asahi Evening News* (English translation of the above), 7 September 1994)

This piece of text is about the bugging scandal of the Japanese security police in mid-1990s. The Japanese original article, (21a), states that the public concern was focussed upon whether an impersonal (and naturally inanimate) organisation, *Keisatsu-chō* or the National Police Agency, ordered the bugging, whilst in its English translational counterpart, the author questions the agency, responsibility and intentionality of the individual police officers of higher positions, although the person referential expression *officers on a high echelon* itself does not possess the status as a grammatical 'Agent' in Dik's sense. Also outside the scope of the Functionalists' framework of syntactic agency are the examples observed in (14) and (16), which illustrate the contrast between Calvin Klein as an individual designer and Calvin Klein as a company and that between individual Diet members and 'Nagata-Town', signifying collectively the Japanese political world. In both cases, the Japanese texts employ collective/grouping expressions to refer to the same entities that are depicted in English texts as individual humans who act of their own accords.

In Section 4.4, the opposition between group/collective agency in Japanese and individualistic human agency in English will be considered again in the light of linguistic relativism and from a more socio-culturally oriented point of view. In the meantime, Section 4.3 will re-examine the theoretical background of the linguistic relativity 'hypothesis' with its decline and recent resurgence.

4.3 Linguistic relativity revisited

In 1940, Benjamin Lee Whorf argued: "Our problem is to determine how different languages segregate different essentials out of the same situation" (1956: 162).[6] At the beginning of the 21st century, this is exactly the central concern that this book addresses in the light of such concepts as 'agency' and 'impersonality', which are essential determinants of what is termed as 'mind-styles' or 'world-views' (cf. Fowler 1977: 103 and 106), and it is exactly to investigate the different ways in which human languages segregate different isolates out of the same situation that use has been made of parallel corpus data.

In this context, our task in the current section is to examine (or re-examine) the 'relativistic' viewpoints on the interrelationship between language, thought and culture, which has been revisited in the recent intellectual milieu. Given that this book is focussed on the concrete manifestations of a particular notion in particular languages, and that we regard linguistic relativity as a conceptual 'tool' of some measure here, we will not be able to plunge into a longish discussion on this deeply enchanting topic. In a nutshell, my basic stance in this book is that the so-called 'classical' version of Whorfianism, if accompanied by thorough literature reviews (cf. Lee 1996; Lucy 1992a), turns out to be quite compatible with some major strands of what Levinson refers to as 'neo-Whorfianism' (2003: 301–307) as contrasted with its predecessor. Through disentangling some of the major theoretical debates and confusions, a useful synthesis will emerge, and it will give stronger shape to our later arguments in Section 4.4.

As Gumperz and Levinson (1996:2) summarise, the original idea of linguistic relativity, which is attributable to Humboldt, Boas, Sapir and Whorf, was that "the semantic structures of different languages might be fundamentally incommensurable, with the consequences for the way in which speakers of specific languages might think and act" (see Chapter 1).[7] As for the development of the concept of linguistic relativity in America, contemporary research has centred upon the works of Benjamin Lee Whorf concerning the questions of whether and how diverse languages influence the styles of human thought, and so will our discussions in the current section, although Whorf's studies on American Indian languages extensively drew upon the works of the anthropologists, Franz Boas and Edward Sapir, Whorf's mentor at Yale University.

Before the original form of the so-called 'Sapir-Whorf hypothesis'[8] was thoroughly tested by sufficient empirical data, the surrounding intellectual climate by the 1960s had become entirely unfavourable for the relativists' view on language and thought, with Berlin and Kay's (1969) demonstration of the language-independent saliency of two to eleven 'basic colour terms' as a 'decisive anti-relativist finding', terminating the interest in discussions on linguistic relativity (Lucy 1992a and 1996; Gumperz & Levinson 1996). Despite their misunderstanding of Whorf's position, the impact of Berlin and Kay's work was paramount. Extensive criticism has since been showered on the general 'theory' of Whorfianism (see, for example, Rosch 1977), on Whorf's Hopi data – especially on its apparent lack of tense – (see Longacre 1956; Malotki 1979 and 1983), on 'the great Eskimo vocabulary hoax' (see Pullum 1991), and so forth (Gumperz & Levinson 1996:14–15; Hill 1988:16–17).

However, scholars such as Alford (1981), Hill (1988), Lee (1996) and Lucy (1992a) have argued back that Whorf has been the victim of a good deal of misrepresentation. In the rest of this section, I will introduce significant discussions and documentations in favour of the original – or 'classical' – version of linguistic relativism, mainly following Hill (1988), Lee (1996) and Lucy (1992a), with supportive empirical evidence from the data provided by Levinson (1997 and 2003), who is obviously one of the most distinguished relativists of today and could be even more 'relativist' than Whorf himself. There are two major issues here: (1) Whorf's pursuit of semantic universality, which has often been forgotten or ignored, and (2) the presupposition that there are two different 'versions' of linguistic relativism – the stronger and the weaker.

Firstly, because of the famous – probably, too famous – lines by Benjamin Whorf cited in (22), too much emphasis was placed on the syntactic mould of human thoughts or the grammatical system in each natural language that determines the way in which its speakers would dissect, interpret and explain the outside world, largely disregarding his discussions on both linguistic and non-linguistic issues on semantic, pragmatic and sociolinguistic levels.

(22)   It is the grammatical background of our mother tongue, which includes not only our way of constructing propositions but the way we dissect nature and break up the flux of experience into objects and entities to construct propositions about. (Whorf 1956: 239)

However, as Lucy (1992a: 178) argues, one of the recent changes in the interpretation of Whorfianism is that linguistic relativity – at least in Whorf's version – does not rule out the possibility of discovering semantic universals shared by infinitely varied human linguistic stocks. For example, Whorf argues as follows, when he contrasts visual experience with non-visual experience:

(23)   Visual experience is projected and constitutes space, or what we shall call the external field of the observer; unvisual experience is introjected and makes up what we shall call, following some Gestalt psychologists, the ego field, or egoic field, because the observer or ego feels himself, as it were, alone with these sensations and awarenesses. Hence in referring a certain experience to the egoic field, because it is not in the visual field, or to the ambivalent borderland, as when a sensation is known by both modes as within the observer's body, we are classing it as all observers class it, regardless of their language, once they understand the nature of the distinction. Moreover, the egoic field has its own Gestalt laws, of sense quality, rhythm, etc., which are universal. (Whorf 1956: 164)

In fact, Whorf himself argued that all groups of humans perceive the environment in essentially the same way as a function of external and internal perceptual processes (Lee 1996: 27–28). Also, his frequent use of such phrases as 'all observers' or 'Mr. Everyman' clearly illustrates Whorf's orientation to cognitive universality.

It is vital to note that Berlin and Kay's (1969) arguments, which once badly obscured the importance of the linguistic relativity hypothesis, were actually based on a somewhat flawed standpoint. Lucy (1992a) points out as follows:

(24)   They [Berlin and Kay] were interested in contesting the claim "associated in America with the names of Edward Sapir and B. L. Whorf" that "the search for semantic universals is fruitless in principle" because "each language is semantically arbitrary relative to every other language" (1969: 2). They maintained that they had refuted this view by showing the existence of a semantic universal precisely in the area of research typically used to exemplify linguistic relativity: "the alleged total semantic arbitrariness of the lexical coding of color" (1969: 2). (Lucy 1992a: 177)

Berlin and Kay stated that all languages operate with two to eleven 'basic colour terms' with apparent limitations on their co-distributions, examples in English being red, green, blue, etc. Lucy argues that since their research was originally designed to identify the sources of linguistic form but not to show the influence of language on thought, Berlin and Kay did not really assess human thought non-linguistically (1992a:178). Indeed, Berlin and Kay's research did not address Whorf's actual proposals or evidence: first and foremost, Whorf did not deny the possibility of discovering semantic universals, and, secondly, the tradition of colour research did not originate with Whorf's works (Lucy 1992a:178–179).

Furthermore, according to Lee, at the ontological core of the linguistic relativity *a la* Benjamin Whorf are (1) the fact of patternment in linguistic and indeed all cultural behaviour and (2) the unequivocal treatment of language as a cognitive activity and as a product of linguistic socialisation (1996:29). This means that Whorf did not observe particular patternings in the linguistic organisation of propositions and in all other human cultural behaviours in a particular linguistic community as the product of the static 'grammatical background' of the native language, as it has been always assumed, but that he had a more up-to-date sociolinguistic standpoint concerning the process of human linguistic enculturation.

As Whorf originally intended, the realm of arguments in the current research ranges from structural or syntactic factors to socio-cultural ones, the latter still awaiting our full attention until the following section. Recognising different levels of universality and relativity is particularly important in our discussions on the linguistic manifestations of 'agency'. Indeed, as I have suggested in Chapter 1, the possibility of discovering semantic, pragmatic and sociolinguistic (or sociocultural) universality implies yet another and quite converse possibility of discovering semantic, pragmatic and sociolinguistic/socio-cultural relativity, along with syntactic relativity (cf. Yamamoto 2000). After all, relativity and universality do not preclude each other. Levinson even argues: "In short, universals that allow variants (and few do not) are completely compatible with 'Whorfianism'" (2003:315). As far as the relativity on a socio-cultural level is concerned, it seems important to remind ourselves of Boas' (1911) concept of 'cultural relativism', which I introduced in Chapter 1. When transcribing and translating native Amerindian texts, Franz Boas acquired the idea that each individual culture must be understood in its own terms but not within the intellectual 'master plan' of 'familiar languages of Europe'; this point of view will also be effective when observing Japanese language and culture, which in many ways make sharp contrast to those in Europe and North America.

One case to illustrate the interrelation between language and thought is, of course, the above-mentioned contrast between the English and Japanese ways of encoding human agency. It must be noted that the different manifestations of potentially agentive human entities, that we have examined in both Chapter 3 and

Section 4.2, do not only stem from the difference in syntactic structures, but are largely concerned with the difference in semantic, pragmatic and socio-cultural connotation of 'agency' – or, under a different guise, inner representations of the agency concept – between these two languages.

Secondly, in the recent past, linguists have been engaged in debates over two quite different 'versions' of Whorfian 'hypotheses', i.e. a stronger form of relativity that presupposes linguistic determinism and a weaker, restricted version that does not. On the one hand, the stronger form of linguistic relativity, or linguistic determinism, is a hypothesis proposing that the forms of language are prior to and determinative of the particular styles of human knowledge and understanding; that is, it asserts that human beings cannot even imagine a kind of knowledge that is not encoded in their language. On the other hand, the weaker form of Whorfianism suggests that "there are no *a priori* constraints on the meanings which a human language might encode, and these encodings will shape unreflective understanding by speakers of a language" (Hill 1988: 15).[9]

It seems quite obvious that a rather 'deterministic' tone reflected in the above-cited lines by Whorf (see (22)) could be one of the major factors which led a host of researchers into believing that linguistic determinism is the very essence of Whorfianism and triggered the swing of the pendulum – linguistic relativity has long been labelled as a rather 'dangerous' doctrine, under the influence of the 'rationalism' and extreme 'universalism' mainly held by the generative linguists.[10] However, it must be recognised that no strong form of linguistic determinism is supported either in the writings of Sapir or Whorf, or in their data (Hill 1988; Lee 1996; Lucy 1992a), and that Whorf acknowledged the existence of non-linguistic thought and knowledge despite the claims by later scholars, as clearly demonstrated in his lines quoted in (23) above (Whorf 1956: 164).

With linguistic determinism largely discredited, recent empirical researches have been centred on testing the second, 'weaker' type of Whorfianism, including the hypothesis that human languages are highly variable, and that this variability is reflected in non-linguistic knowledge and behaviour (Hill 1988: 16). The core of the 'Whorfian theory complex' can be represented by the two fundamental questions, which are found in the following extract:

(25)   That portion of the whole investigation here to be reported may be summed up in two questions: (1) Are our own concepts of 'time,' 'space,' and 'matter' given in substantially the same form by experience to all men, or are they in part conditioned by the structure of particular languages? (2) Are there traceable affinities between (a) cultural and behavioral norms and (b) large-scale linguistic patterns?   (Whorf 1956: 138)

There are clear indications in these questions that Whorf's chief concern was the connection between certain aspects of natural languages and those of the 'habitual thought world' of their native speakers (Lucy 1992a: 39 and 62; Lee 1996: 29), which has previously been referred to, under a different guise, as 'mind-style' or 'world-view'. It naturally follows, then, that the 'second version' of linguistic relativity is actually what Whorfian principles were originally about. Lucy (1992a: 307) even argues that, contrary to widespread belief (cf. Rosch 1977), works of serious investigators cannot be readily divided into the stronger ('language determines') and weaker ('language influences') versions of the hypothesis.

As Levinson (2003: 18) argues, in the main-stream trend of modern linguistics, any evidence for even the restricted or 'weaker' version of linguistic relativity has been treated with a great deal of scepticism. However, there are indeed many ac-tual observations of the affinity between the large-scale linguistic patterns found in particular languages and the distinctive, habitual styles of thinking shared by their native speakers (cf. Gumperz & Levinson 1996; Nuyts & Pederson 1997, *inter alia*). On top of the comparative studies of Benjamin Whorf himself on the ha-bitual thought worlds in English, Hopi, Shawnee, etc., that are co-ordinated with their wide-spread linguistic features, one of the excellent cases in point amongst recent findings is Stephen Levinson's observation of the spatial description and conception in the Tzeltal language (or one of its dialects). We shall examine here some of his striking findings.

Tzeltal is a Mayan language spoken in Chiapas, Mexico. The specific dialect of Tzeltal Levinson studied is the one spoken in the highlands in Tenejapa by the people called the Tenejapans, but for the sake of simplicity, the Tenejapan dialect will simply be referred to as 'Tzeltal' (Levinson 1997: 34). The geographical back-ground information of the highlands is of great importance and relevance in dis-cussing the connection between the linguistic characteristics of Tzeltal and the way in which its native speakers' habitual thought world (or mind-style/world-view) is constructed. Levinson explains:

(26)   Tenejapa is an upland *municipio* in highland Chiapas, Mexico, located in
        rugged country ranging in elevation from about 2,000 metres to under 1,000
        metres, and thus ecologically from subalpine pine forest to tropical condi-
        tions. Overall, the territory forms an incline from high south to low north,
        cut by many deep valleys. In this territory live speakers of a dialect of Tzeltal.
        … The c. 15,000 inhabitants practise slash-and-burn maize and bean cultiva-
        tion, as their ancestors have for well over a thousand years.

                                                                    (Levinson 2003: 146)

Tzeltal is a language that lacks the notions of 'right', 'left', 'front' and 'back' – the 'egocentric' or 'relative' parameters of spatial descriptions that are prevalent in many languages in the world, including English and Japanese, for instance. Instead of such relative co-ordinates, Tzeltal utilises 'absolute' co-ordinates together with a rich system of 'intrinsic' distinctions (Levinson 1994; Brown 1994); the use of 'intrinsic' indicators of space directions is to be illustrated in the example below:

(27) *Waxal*   *ta*   **x-chikin** *mexa te   p'ine.*
      Stand:of:vertical:cylinder PREP its-ear   table the pot.
      'The pot is standing at the corner of the table'.   (Levinson 2003:147)

Marked in boldface, we can see the use of intrinsic topological system, employing body-part terms, such as 'ear' (Levinson 2003:147). However, our focus here falls not on this 'intrinsic' system of space description but on the 'absolute' system, which seems more influential than the former upon the 'habitual thought world' of the Tzeltals. Levinson maintains as follows:

(28) Tzeltal cardinal directions are not directly related to celestial phenomena but are derived from characteristics of the landscape: the term that corresponds to (somewhat east of) north means literally 'down' and relates to the steep drop of Tenejapan territory from an alpine southern range to a tropical northern river valley. We will gloss the term as 'downhill'; 'uphill' therefore corresponds to a southerly direction. The orthogonal directions east and west are covered by the one term which we gloss as 'across'. . . .   (Levinson 1997:35)

The absolute system of space description and conception in Tzeltal involves an idealised plane, abstracted from the native speakers' familiar landscape. The directions across this plane are designated *ajk'ol* 'uphill (roughly south)', *alan* 'downhill (roughly north)' and *jejch* 'across (either east or west)' (Levinson 2003:148), and, surprisingly, the speakers of this language are able to designate the location of any entity on earth in terms of these absolute co-ordinates. If, for instance, someone asks the location of a bottle, in relation to that of a chair, one could reply as in:

(29) *Waxal*   *ta*   **y-ajk'ol** *xila   te   limite.*
      Stand:of:vertical:cylinder PREP its-uphill chair the bottle.
      'The bottle is standing uphill (i.e. south) of the chair'.
                                                              (Levinson 2003:148)

According to Levinson, even more surprising is the fact that the Tenejapans are always able to locate their cardinal directions without difficulty. They do not need to view the actual landscape with the incline of their hill, in giving such description as in (29), and "the same locutions would be used in a novel house in the night, and in any case in any actual location", valleys and banks lying in all directions (Levinson 2003:149). In fact, Levinson also argues that native speakers taken outside their territory, from which the inclined plane is abstracted, also utilise "the system fixed compass-like bearings wherever they are" (2003:149). Even if one takes his Tenejapan subjects into an unfamiliar concrete cell without windows and asks them to point to places to which they have been at the distance of 100 miles away, they can accurately point in the correct direction (Levinson 1997:35). Indeed, in this community of the Tenejapans, verbal communication would fail without their special 'magnetic' sense of cardinal directions.

One of the most prominent points made out of this investigation into the Tzeltal language is that it seems to be the Tenejapan's peculiar cognitive ability of perceiving the cardinal directions that facilitates the peculiar characteristics of this language – the lack of the notions of relative co-ordinates of spatial description, i.e. those of 'right', 'left', 'front' and 'back', and not vice versa. In other words, it seems to be the case that the Tzeltal thought world, which enables its native speakers to locate the cardinal directions wherever they are, influences the large-scale patterns of their language.

This further implies that the causal relation between language and thought is (at least) bilateral. As many have argued, widely found linguistic patterns of a certain natural language can often influence the thought world shared by its native speakers, but it can be otherwise as in the case of the Tzeltal spatial cognition. If the grammatical patterns of one's native language do always determine its speakers' style of thinking, as an imaginary language determinist of the old school would have argued, then how could the Tenejapans have acquired in the first place their special sense of absolute spatial co-ordinates? It is difficult to believe that their peculiar ability of telling the cardinal directions came after the surface linguistic patterns of their mother tongue.

Having determined that the affinity between the large-scale linguistic patterns in a natural language and its native speakers' habitual ways of thinking is bilateral, we need to introduce the third element that constitutes the core of Whorfianism – i.e. 'culture' – on top of 'language' and 'thought'. It was Whorf himself who broached the potential connection between language patterns and cultural patterns, which had actually been rejected by his predecessors Boas and Sapir (Lucy 1992a:63). The second part of Whorf's fundamental questions mentioned above is: "Are there traceable affinities between (a) cultural and behavioral norms and (b) large-scale linguistic patterns?" (Whorf 1956:138). He also maintained:

> (30)   There are connections . . . between cultural norms and linguistic patterns. Although it would be impossible to infer the existence of Crier Chief[11] from the lack of tenses in Hopi, or vice versa, there is a relation between a language and the rest of the culture of the society which uses it. There are cases where the "fashions of speaking" are closely integrated with the whole general culture, whether or not this be universally true . . . .   (Whorf 1956:159)

Whorf tried to figure out an indirect connection wherein language influences culture in some cases via its effect on the habitual thought world of its speakers (Lucy 1992a:63). Lucy schematises the manner how specific linguistic patterns influence native speakers' thought, which then in the end stimulate the devel-

Large-scale linguistic patterns
(= integrated fashions of speaking)
↓1
Linguistically conditioned habitual thought world
(= microcosm that each man carries about within himself)
↓2
Linguistically conditioned features of culture
(= cultural and behavioural norms)

Figure 2. Structures of Whorf's argument linking language, the individual and culture (based on Lucy 1992a: 64)

opment of particular cultural institutions as in Figure 2. Note that, in Whorf's terminology, the 'habitual thought world' of the speakers of a certain language is the "microcosm that each man carries about within himself" (Whorf 1956: 147).

It is interesting to note here that 'thought' or, more precisely, 'habitual thought world' shared by the speakers of a particular natural language constitutes the 'intermediate' level, that links the large-scale linguistic patterns and the cultural/behavioural norms of a specific linguistic community. What we should be careful about with the above figure is the direction of arrows 1 and 2 connecting these three layers. As has been demonstrated through Levinson's documentation of the Tzeltal language, arrow 1 in Figure 2 must be bilateral, not unilateral. This seems to be the case with the relation between 'language' and 'culture' and, naturally, that between 'thought' and 'culture' (see the arrow 2 in the figure). Whorf was careful throughout in characterising the nature of the connection between language and the rest of culture, which, interestingly, he characterised as a kind of 'assemblage of norms', and did not assert a necessary causal relation between them (Lucy 1992a: 65). In the following quotation, he construes that this affinity is *principally* of bilateral nature involving a certain 'chicken-and-egg dilemma', that I mentioned at the very beginning of this chapter:

(31)   How does such a network of language, culture, and behavior come about historically? Which was first: the language patterns or the cultural norms? In main they have grown up together, constantly influencing each other.

(Whorf 1956: 156)

Cultural theorists' point of view on these connections is that, according to Hill (1988: 18), 'culture' is to be seen as a set of 'complexly rational' mental phenomena, consisting of (1) a hierarchy of rules concerning the construction of propositions, that is so pervasive and hence 'undiscussable' by the natives, and (2) a set of descriptive and normative propositions. We can argue that this view comes to terms with what has been discussed above following Whorf: culture involves both a propositional or linguistic meaning system and a set of behavioural norms. Given that the relationship between 'language' and 'culture' – via the intermediate factor of 'thought' – is bilateral, there is a possibility that language itself sometimes responds to the pressure of cultural (or, more precisely, socio-cultural) norms. This will actually be proved to be the case in the following section through the manifestation (or non-manifestation) of agency in Japanese honorifics.

The thesis drawn from our re-examination of Whorf's works that the affinities amongst 'language', 'thought' and 'culture' are bilateral seems to be compatible with the very essence of what is dubbed as 'neo-Whorfianism' (Levinson 2003). 'Neo-Whorfianism' is the term with which Stephen Levinson (2003: 302–307) refers to the most recent resurgence of interest in Whorfian ideas with converging strands of thought from different fields such as philosophy, linguistic anthropology and developmental psychology, his own research into the Tzeltal spatial expressions being one of the manifestations of such new strands.

Levinson regards the original, 'classical' version of Whorfianism as somewhat faulty and advances a limited kind of Whorfian idea that "human spatial thinking is quite heavily influenced by culture, and more specifically by language", and that "when languages differ in crucial respects, so does the corresponding conceptualization of spatial relations" (2003: 18). He criticises Whorf's works, arguing that Whorf interpreted "the influence of language on thought to inhere in an entrainment of 'habitual thought'", and that such an entrainment is an "insidious" one. Levinson further maintains that the neo-Whorfian perspectives, which emerges afresh from, for instance, his case studies on Tzeltal, are not (classically) Whorfian in any strict sense, since the new approach does not emphasise "the role that obligatory grammatical categories have on particular patterns of thinking", as Benjamin Whorf did (Levinson 2003: 301).

However, it seems quite important to remember here that old, original form of Whorfianism was not as faulty as Levinson construes. As has been argued earlier, Whorf himself did not wish to assert a necessary causal relation between the large-scale linguistic characteristics of a particular natural language and the habitual thought patterns pervasively shared by its native speakers, recognising this connection as principally bilateral in nature with a hint of a chicken-and-egg dilemma (cf. Lucy 1992a: 65). In fact, in terms of the three-layered structure of the linkage between 'language', 'thought' and 'culture' as represented in Figure 2, Levinson's point that "human spatial thinking is quite heavily influenced by culture, and more specifically by language", and that "when languages differ in crucial respects, so does the corresponding conceptualization of spatial relations" (2003: 18) also suggests the bilateral nature of the affinities between these three basic human inheritances. In this sense, the neo-Whorfian perspectives can be quite 'Whorfian' in an original sense. It can be also argued that, as it is clear from our preceding discussions on Whorf's original research interests, Whorf himself was not solely focussing upon "the role that obligatory grammatical categories have on particular patterns of thinking".

Nonetheless, Levinson's contribution to the advancement of the linguistic relativity principles is paramount, with his significant case studies suggestive of the bilateral symmetry of the co-relation between 'language', 'thought' and 'culture', which (ironically, perhaps) makes his ideas completely compatible with those of Whorf. However, there are of course some novelties which place the neo-Whorfian account of language, thought and culture on a higher plane than its ancestor; amongst the most notable of such advancements is the introduction of 'memory' as a focal point.

Levinson's conclusive argument on three distinct types of Whorfian effects is quite straightforward, the first and second types being theoretically uncontested (2003: 302–303). The first type of 'Whorfian effects' is concerned with 'coding' after speaking: "the fact that thoughts have already been coded linguistically may affect the way they are recollected, categorised or used in inference" (Levinson 2003: 302). Secondly, there are such effects that operate at the very moment of utterance. "At the moment of linguistic coding, thoughts have to be regimented to fit the lexical, grammatical and linear structure of the particular language" (Levinson 2003: 303); this is what Slobin (1996) terms 'thinking-for-speaking'.

Finally, there comes what Levinson refers to as 'experiencing for speaking', where "events at the moment of experience must be coded in terms appropriate for later expression in the local language" (Levinson 2003: 303). This argument is still quite controversial, Levinson argues, but it can be supported by Lucy's (1992b) account of number distinction in Yucatec, another Mayan language. Lucy (1992b) compared native speakers of English, which requires obligatory number marking, to those of Yucatec, which requires its nouns of no number distinction, producing in effect sentences like *There be bird in the garden*. He argues that when reporting an event, Yucatec speakers do not describe number, and that they remember things with less specificity about number than English native speakers (Lucy 1992b). Out of Lucy's findings, Levinson construes that any natural language that forces language-specific coding of events – such as English with its obligate number distinction – "will require its speakers to remember those relevant parameters at the time at which events are experienced" (2003: 302). This of course fortifies the view that 'language' and 'thought' are clearly intertwined with each other and leads to one of Levinson's conclusive arguments that 'semantic parameters' are not universal, that is, not shared by all languages (2003: 302). This last point makes us conclude that Levinson is even more 'relativistic' than Whorf himself, in that, whereas the latter stressed the importance of semantic universality behind the surface, grammatical differences amongst natural languages of various stocks, the former argues for the non-universality of certain 'semantic parameters' such as number distinction, the expression of deference and respect (cf. Levinson's arguments on Japanese and Javanese honorifics in 2003: 302), etc.

Having determined that 'neo-Whorfianism' is quite compatible with its predecessor, it is natural to assume that typically Whorfian research methods may well be still valid. In fact, Lucy argues that Whorf's research not only served as the historical point of departure for our review of linguistic relativity, but "still presents the most adequate empirical approach" to the issues that represent the correlation between language, thought and culture (1992a: 257). In concluding this section, we shall take a brief look at the methodological aspect of Whorfianism and ascertain that the method of our empirical research in this book is compatible with it.

In terms of the collection and analysis of actual data for his empirical research, Whorf adopted a contrastive point of view, basically comparing the semantic structures of *two* languages and then tracing connections between such meaning structures and various cultural beliefs. "Individual thought was inferred from the language analysis and empirically verified by reference to related cultural patterns of belief and behavior" (Lucy 1992a: 258). In this book, the data collected through the parallel corpora in two languages – i.e. Japanese and English – is analysed contrastively with reference to the semantic (or conceptual) parameter of 'agency', which happens to be shared between the languages in question, unlike the above-mentioned case of number distinction in English and Yucatec (Lucy 1992b). The general tendencies regarding the expression and suppression of human agency in Japanese and English have already been examined to a considerable extent, but the part of 'tracing connections' between the characteristics of encoding agency in these languages and various cultural beliefs and institutions in the Japanese and English speaking cultures is still to follow. So here we go.

4.4 Agency, impersonality, mind-styles and cultural norms

One of the theses drawn from the previous section is that the co-relations between large-scale linguistic patternings, (linguistically affected) habitual thought worlds and behavioural and cultural norms are bilateral, and this implies that the boundaries between these three elements can be rather hazy, with the possibility that they may sometimes merge. Indeed, as Levinson (2003) construes, 'language' is to be regarded as an important aspect of 'culture'. One's 'habitual thought world' can also be one form of the 'culture' to which he/she belongs and thus mirrors certain aspects of one's 'behavioural and cultural norms'.

In this section, the fruit of the re-examination of the Whorfian ideas of linguistic relativity (as well as that of the examination of 'neo-Whorfianism') will be integrated with our findings on the manifestations of agency in English and

Japanese, that I have presented in Chapter 3 and Section 4.2. Oversimplifying our preceding discussions, we can argue that the 'large-scale linguistic patterning' in question in the current context is that, on the one hand, English tends to articulate (individual) human agency through the use of person referential expressions, but that, on the other hand, Japanese tends to considerably suppress or obfuscate it in making person reference, with the impersonality concept looming over. This is the case both within the syntactic framework proposed by the Functional Grammarian, Simon Dik, and outside such structural limitation – i.e. in terms of more semantically and pragmatically oriented views on agency and impersonality.

In Section 4.4.1, the above-mentioned propensities in the two languages will be associated with more general points of view on human (animate) entities as a part of both the habitual thought patterns (or mind-styles/world-views) and the representative cultural norms of the Japanese- and English-speaking world. Section 4.4.2 focuses upon the co-relationship between the Japanese and English ways of encoding 'agency' and the conflicting concepts of individualism and collectivism, probing the widely-held socio-cultural norms and values in these distinctive linguistic communities.

4.4.1 Treatment of human entities

What can we find behind the 'large-scale linguistic patterns' at issue, i.e. (1) the propensity for the impersonal expression (or suppression) of agency in Japanese and (2) the clear, articulate encoding of human agency in English? First of all, we will tackle this question in terms of habitual styles of thinking and then in terms of cultural and behavioural norms. Our chief concern in this subsection will be about the different varieties of world-views/mind-styles concerning the interpretation and treatment of human entities.

According to our previous observations and discussions, there are (at least) three fashions in which human agents can be impersonalised: (1) 'positionalisation' or 'locationalisation' of persons, (2) complete effacement of human elements overwhelmingly through ellipsis and (3) expressing individual humans as a part of a group or a collective mass. These are not patents of the Japanese language and can of course be observed in English too, as argued in Chapter 2 through Fairclough *et al.*'s examples; however, the result of case studies using parallel corpus data has shown that the occurrence of such impersonality phenomena is far more frequent in Japanese than in English. The current subsection is concerned with the first two issues above, and the last problem of group/collective agency will be revisited in 4.4.2 but with a considerable bias towards examples in Japanese.

As far as the phenomena of 'positionalisation of persons' are concerned, we have seen examples like the following in the Japanese texts within the parallel corpora: the designer, Calvin Klein, expressed as a venue where particular kinds of clothes are designed and produced, the anger of Russian officials expressed as the anger of the entire nation, one's relatives expressed through the name of the city where they live, etc. A rather metaphorical form of 'positionalisation of persons', that is prevalent in Japanese, is making person reference through the common noun phrases designating one's occupations and social standings including kinship terms, which impersonalise human referents by 'clothing' them with their roles and functions.

The habitual patterns of thinking behind these surface linguistic phenomena in Japanese is, quite simply, to interpret personal, human entities as impersonal 'positions', that can be either spatial or social; it is natural that such dehumanised human entities are to be deprived of their agency, responsibility, intentionality, etc. This has further socio-cultural implications in the Japanese-speaking society, with a human entity as a 'locus' representing a certain 'cultural and behavioural norm', which can be most clearly illustrated in the use of a particular type of honorifics. As it has been argued in Section 4.3 following Levinson (2003:302), honorifics can be characterised as one of the 'semantic parameters' which are not universally observed in natural languages over the world and hence as a notable phenomenon representing one form of socio-cultural as well as linguistic relativity.

Consider the following honorific sentence in Japanese and its English translation:

(32) a. *Tennō-heika   ni-okase-rare-mashite-wa,*   *ine   no   nae   o*
          Emperor   at-HON-TOP,   rice LK seedling ACC
          o-ue-ni-nari-mashi-ta.
          plant-HON-PAST.

      b. The Emperor planted rice seedlings.   (cf. Ikegami 1991:314)

Through the above example, Ikegami (1991) illustrates an exceptionally revealing phenomenon in Japanese, where a potentially agentive (or 'Agentive' in the Functional Grammarians' terms) participant is encoded as a 'satellite' entity for the sake of deference. (32a) is an ideal example of 'positionalisation of persons'; a special honorific construction allows (or orders) a Japanese speaker/writer to avoid encoding the agency of the Emperor, expressing him as if he were a certain location where the action of planting rice seedlings took place. Since attributions of agency can sometimes mean accusations or assignments of responsibility (cf. Davidson 1971:9 and also our previous discussions in Chapter 2), overtly expressing someone's agency (and animacy) may have a face threatening effect. Therefore, expressing the Emperor as a very personal and agentive entity is regarded as a linguistic taboo in the Japanese-speaking culture (cf. Yamamoto 1999:173). Conversely, the English sentence in (32b) clearly encodes the agency of the Emperor, who occupies the position of a grammatical Agent; however, this does not cause any face threatening effect.

'Honorific' person reference in Japanese such as the one in (32a) can naturally be interpreted as constituting one of many 'large-scale linguistic patterns' in this language and hence is concerned with the 'linguistic' level in the three-layered schematic strata of linguistic relativity; however, it represents, at the same time, a 'code' of Japanese cultural and behavioural norms, that is imprinted in the 'habitual thought world' of fully-socialised adult native speakers of this language. As we have argued at the beginning of this section, the boundaries between the three levels of 'language', 'thought' and 'culture' can be rather hazy, and these three elements merge with one another into a complex of honorifics.

In Japanese, deference and respect can be closely associated with the concept of 'impersonality', and 'positionalisation of persons' in a metaphorical, 'social' sense plays an important part. Making person reference through common noun phrases designating one's social positions, statuses, kinship terms, etc. often conveys a sense of politeness to the addressee and referent, particularly when the position he/she holds is supposed to be a superior or important one. Accordingly, it can be argued that the pervasive use of role terms in Japanese directly reflects the cultural/behavioural norm and the hierarchical mind-style that facilitate speakers to encode deference and respect in referring to human entities, especially those whose social standings are relatively 'high' (cf. Section 4.2). For instance, one of the basic socio-cultural norms regarding the use of kinship terms in Japanese is that only those terms denoting older members in the family than oneself – e.g. *o-tō-san* ('father'), *o-kā-san* ('mother'), *o-nī-san/o-nī-chan/nī-san* ('elder brother'), *o-nē-san/o-nē-chan/nē-san* ('elder sister'), *o-jī-chan* ('grandfather'), *o-bā-chan* ('grandmother'), etc. – can be used as forms of address (for more details, see Suzuki 1978).

The following example which we examined earlier clearly illustrates the case where the writer of the Japanese original text conveys a sense of respect to the then Prime Minister, Tomiichi Murayama, by keeping referring to him as *shushō* ('prime minister'), whilst the corresponding English translation does not, using personal pronouns after the first mention and hence expressing this man simply as a 'human male'.

(33) a. *Murayama Tomiichi* <u>*shushō*</u>   *ga*   *Azia yon-ka-koku*   *no*
          Murayama Tomiichi <u>prime:minister</u> NOM Asia four-countries LK

          Ø   *tabi o   oe-ta.*
          (his) trip ACC finish-PAST.

> _Shushō_   _wa_   _kono rekihō de,_   Ø   _nerai-to-shi-ta Azia_
> Prime:minister NOM this   visit   by, (he) aim-PART   Asia
> _jūshi_   _no shisei_   _o,_   _mazu-wa_
> attach:ing:importance LK attitude ACC, in:the:first:place
> _shime-se-ta_   _no-de-wa-nai-ka._
> show-can-PAST AUX.

(Text 3: Asahi Shimbun, 31 August 1994)

> b. <u>Prime Minister</u> Tomiichi Murayama has completed <u>his</u> visit to four coun-
> tries in Asia. <u>He</u> may be said to have shown to Asian leaders how much
> importance Japan attaches to Asian countries, as <u>he</u> has intended, during
> <u>his</u> trip.   (Text 3: Asahi Evening News, 31 August 1994)

Yet another aspect of what can be termed as 'common NP mind-style' can be observed through rather unusual examples in English as in (34):

(34)   a.   Your supervisor is Margaret Deuchar, isn't it?
       b.   They accused him of being a horrible schoolmaster, which he was.
       c.   She isn't the brilliant wrestler that she used to be.

In (34a), a common noun phrase designating a human entity, i.e. the expression your supervisor, is treated as inanimate with the inanimate pronoun it in the tag. It can be construed that the speaker does not imbue 'your supervisor' with ani-macy, assuming that being a supervisor of one research student is one 'position' in the Department. The sentences in (34b) and (34c) also illustrate the case where common noun phrases impersonalise human referents, coupled with the use of impersonal relative pronouns which and that (cf. Yamamoto 1999: 34). However, it must be stressed that this inanimate use of common human noun phrases is ex-tremely rare in English, whereas the Japanese language often makes use of it; the only reason why we needed English examples here is that the inanimate nature of these referential expressions can be highlighted more clearly in English simply because of their correspondence with inanimate pronouns, which can never be observed in Japanese.

In terms of the concept of 'cultural norms', in Japanese society, social roles themselves (including social positions and statuses) represent particular be-havioural patterns or norms which one is expected to (or sometimes even forced to) acquire or follow in a particular socio-cultural frame (cf. our previous discus-sions in Section 4.2). For Japanese individuals, 'roles' are ends in themselves, and one is expected to alter oneself to suit a particular role to which he/she is assigned (Minoura 1991: 115).

The articulation and suppression of agency in English and Japanese respec-tively can be strong drive for their characteristic manners of making person reference; in particular, the problem of positionalisation of human entities has large-scale repercussions onto the whole system of person reference in the Japanese language. As we have observed through a variety of examples from the corpus data, it is the case that, in order to encode human elements in terms of either spatial or social 'positions', person reference is to be made by common noun phrases, but not by personal pronouns,[12] that constitute a complicated network of a large number of 'semi-content words', despite their infrequent occurrences (cf. Yamamoto 1999: 76–84). As shown in Section 4.2, out of 441 common noun phrases in the Japanese texts (Texts 1 to 6 in the parallel corpora), 34 noun phrases (7.71% of the total number of common noun phrases) correspond to English personal and possessive pronouns. However, there is only one English common noun phrase designating a social role of a human entity (0.22%), out of the total of 455, whose Japanese equivalent is a personal pronoun. On the one hand, personal pronouns usually encode truly 'personal' information, but, on the other hand, common noun phrases encode information about various different aspects of an individual human entity and assign a unique referent to a class of similar referents in terms of what they do and what they have relative to particular positions in a community (cf. Miller & Johnson-Laird 1976: 301–302). Impersonalisation and positionalisation of human entities constitute important facets of what can be dubbed as the 'common NP mind-style' reflected in the Japanese ways of person reference.

In general accounts of features of personal pronouns, excluding inanimate third person pronouns, the kinds of information that they tend to encode consist of very basic, core information about the nature of their referents as human/animate beings (cf., for instance, Quirk, Greenbaum, Leech, & Svartvik 1985; Mühlhäusler & Harré 1990). In other words, singular personal pronouns tend to present their referents as 'bare human/animate beings' with 'bare personal existence', whereas common noun phrases designating humans – say, kinship terms and those words designating one's occupation and social status – 'clothe' the individuals with certain positions or roles. It naturally follows, then, that personal pronouns may have somewhat 'censurable' characteristics; it is mainly because of this rather 'taboo' and potentially 'face threatening' nature of personal pronouns that their use is limited in Japanese.

Yamamoto (1999: Chs. 3 and 4) argues that, unlike a common noun phrase, a (singular) personal pronoun can refer to an individual as a 'whole' person, whereas common noun phrases (and even proper names!) tend to capture limited aspects of the same individual. Consider the following examples in English, where the use of personal pronouns is the unmarked behavioural norms in making coreference:

(35)   I quite like *her* as *a colleague* and *she*'s very pleasant as *a casual friend* but *she* is impossible to live with.   (Brown & Yule 1983: 56)

(36)   During *her* years as *Mrs. Onassis, she*'d slip into Madison Avenue boutiques to
        snap up *her* signature turtlenecks, usually one in every color.

(Text 4: Newsweek, 29 August 1994)

The personal pronouns *she* and *her* in (35) capture the referent as a 'whole', 'full-
bodied' human being. The scope of these personal pronouns comprise both those
aspects of this individual human entity as *a colleague* and *a casual friend* and many
other different aspects including those which make it impossible for the speaker to
live with this person.

  Example (36) was found in a magazine article on the revival of the fashion *a
la* Jacqueline Kennedy Onassis in the mid-1990s and illustrates a somewhat unusual case where even 'names' do not refer to an individual as a 'whole' person.[13]
Here, the name *Mrs. Onassis* encodes a role and position of this person during her
particular period of life. The same is true with the previous name of this individual, *Mrs. Kennedy*, which was almost synonymous with the common noun phrase
the President's wife in the certain period of history of the United States. However,
what is striking with the personal pronouns *she* and *her* is that they can cross the
span of the life of an individual human entity and can continue to refer to the same
person as a 'whole' human being throughout (Yamamoto 1999:133). This very nature of personal pronouns constitutes a very important part of what we can term
as 'pronominal mind-style' – i.e. a pronominal way of habitual thinking – which
is pervasive in English-speaking minds, but seems hardly acceptable to Japanese-
speaking minds, in which the avoidance of FTAs is of paramount importance for
conforming to their behavioural norms.

  One of the large-scale linguistic manifestations of 'pronominal mind-style'
in English is the generic use of personal pronouns. Consider again the following
extract from Mishima's *Hyaku-man Yen Sembei*:

(37)   a.   "... *Kōyū tokoro wa, hitotsu hitotsu wa yasui yō demo,*
            "... Such place TOP, one   one   TOP cheap seem though,
            kekkyoku omoigake-nai o-kane o tsuka-waseru yō-ni
            eventually unexpected   money ACC spend-cause:PART as
            deki-teru   n-da-mono".
            made-PART COP".

(Text 1: Yukio Mishima, Hyaku-man Yen Sembei)

       b.   "... Everything seems so cheap, but it's all arranged so that [you spend
            more money than you intend to]".

(Text 1: English translation of the above)

The use of the second person pronoun *you* in the English translational passage in
(37b) is particularly noteworthy. Both the first and second *you* here are the grammatical Agents of the embedded clauses marked with square brackets and encode

the agency of the (potential) customers without referring to any particular individual human entities, but with an implication that such unknown mass of people must be like the addressee, who is the speaker's husband. Whilst the generic use of second person personal pronouns as found in the above case is quite a widespread phenomenon in English, none of such instances can be found in the Japanese texts in the parallel corpora. When the identity of a potential actor is indefinite, a generic personal pronoun can used as a 'dummy' Agent (Yamamoto 1999: 170); as argued in Chapter 3, the extensive use of generic personal pronouns can be interpreted as a means of sustaining the 'actor-action pattern' of clause construction in English.

A prominent characteristic of the habitual thought world in the English language can be observed behind the common use of 'dummy' pronominal actors: Benjamin Whorf clearly pointed out that "we are constantly reading into nature fictional acting entities" (1956: 243) in making person reference through generic personal pronouns. Whorf's account of English generic pronouns sheds light upon a conspicuous aspect of the English 'pronominal mind-style', which makes its native speakers habitually "read into nature fictional acting entities". One of the rhetorical manifestations of this propensity for fictional agents is the common use of 'personification' as a figurative means of speech, to which we shall return in Chapter 5.

At this stage, it seems useful to consider the somewhat peculiar characteristics of Japanese 'personal pronouns' here. Generally speaking, Japanese personal pronouns behave in quite the same way as common nouns do, not only in that they can be modified by determiners and relative clauses, but in the sense that they embrace a wide range of lexical forms which are to be selected according to the human relationship between speakers, addressees and referents, the relative formality of the speech events concerned and the gender of speech act participants and referents (Yamamoto 1999: 77). In terms of these criteria, Yamamoto (1992a and 1999) classifies the central members of Japanese personal pronouns (singular forms) as shown in Figure 3.

The use of first and second person personal pronouns is susceptible to the gender of the speaker (but not that of the addressee(s)), but the gender distinctions which these terms exhibit are not grammatically obligatory. In Figure 3, when a first and second person item is followed by the signs either (F) or (M), this means that such a pronoun is used by female speakers or male speakers respectively. If a particular form is used by both female and male speakers, it is followed by both (F) and (M); when (M) precedes (F), this means that the pronoun is more likely to be used by male speakers than female speakers. Where (F) precedes (M), female speakers are more likely to use the form in question than male speakers. As for the third person personal pronouns, (M) and (F) indicate the genders of referents (but not those of speakers or addressees). Figure 3 is not clearly divided by vertical

		formal/polite	FORMALITY neutral	informal	stigmatised
P	1	wata(ku)shi (F/M)	boku (M) watashi (F)	ore (M) atashi (F) uchi(F)	washi (M)
E					
R					
S	2	anata (F/M)	anata (F) o-taku (F/M)	kimi (M) omae (M)	kisama (M) temē (M)
O					
N	3		kare (M) kanojo (F)		

Figure 3. Personal pronouns (singular forms) in Japanese (taken from Yamamoto 1999: 78 with slight modifications)

lines in terms of 'formality', because the correlation between the use of particular pronouns and the relative formality of speech events (including topics of conversation) is a matter of gradience and may be different from individual to individual (Yamamoto 1999: 78).

The biggest difference between Japanese and Indo-European languages in terms of the nature of second person personal pronouns is that even the formal and supposedly polite form of *anata* is perceived to be face threatening enough when used to refer to or address a (supposedly) socially 'superior' addressee. Other members of second person personal pronouns in Japanese can be used only when the speakers judge that the referents are either socially 'equal'[14] or 'inferior' to them (for further discussions, see Yamamoto 1999: 115). These facts lead to the taboo-laden nature of second person personal pronouns in general, and it naturally follows, then, that avoidance of such terms on the whole is the safest way according to Japanese behavioural norms. Third person pronouns *kare* ('he') and *kanojo* ('she') – originally place deictic terms meaning 'the man over there' and 'the woman over there' respectively – are actually calques that were introduced after the nineteenth century to translate third person personal pronouns in Western languages, and, even in the present day, their use is imbued with many 'taboo' characteristics. The simplest 'norm' is that they are not normally used to refer to social superiors (for more details, see Hinds 1975: 154; Yamamoto 1999: 122).

In terms of 'positionalisation of persons' and the impersonality concept, two minor members of personal pronouns shown in Figure 3 are of particular interest: a first person pronoun, *uchi*, and a second person pronoun, *o-taku*. The original, literal meanings of *uchi* and *o-taku* are 'my house' (or, in certain cases, 'our house') and 'your house' respectively, and, in this sense, they can be regarded as spatial expressions which encode individual humans as locations (Yamamoto 1999: 144). Extracts (38) and (39) below are not of direct relevance to the agency concept itself but illustrate the use of these pronouns in the parallel corpora, providing good

examples of human entities expressed as 'positions' in Japanese. It should be noted
here that, on the one hand, *uchi* and *o-taku* comfortably impersonalise their human referents to a considerable extent, but that, on the other hand, the equivalent
English pronouns clearly express the referents' personhood and intentionality, although they do not refer to any grammatical Agents. *O-taku* in (39a) corresponds
to an English first person possessive pronoun, because the Japanese translational
clause is in direct speech, whilst the English original is in indirect speech.

(38) a. "...*Demo uchi*   *no   kumiai-in   wa   sonna hanashi o*
          "...But (our)house GEN union-member NOM such story   ACC
          kii-temo fuan-ni   naru   koto-wa-nai"
          hear-if   insecure become NEG"
                              (Text 4: *Newsweek* (Japanese edition), 31 August 1994)

      b. "...But I can't say that the members of <u>our</u> union feel any insecurity
          about the situation"   (Text 4: *Newsweek*, 29 August 1994)

(39) a. "'*O-taku*   *no   seihin   wa   Ø   ka-e-nai*'   *to   Nihon no*
          "'(Your)house GEN product TOP (we) buy-can-NEG' that Japan LK
          kokyaku   kara   Ø   iw-are-ta   koto-ga-aru"
          customer from (I) tell-PASS-PAST once"
                              (Text 4: *Newsweek* (Japanese edition), 31 August 1994)

      b. "I've actually had customers tell me that they couldn't buy <u>our</u> [telecom-
          munications] products here"   (Text 4: *Newsweek*, 29 August 1994)

The use of the pronouns, *uchi* ('(my/our) house') and *o-taku* ('(your) house'), as
the means of first and second person reference illustrates not only the Japanese
habitual thought world, where individual human entities are 'positionalised', but
also its native speakers' collectivistic mind-styles. Etymologically speaking, the expressions '*uchi*' and '*o-taku*' both mean the extension of one's 'house', which is
quite synonymous to the concept of 'family' in Japanese society. In the cases of the
above examples, these pronouns refer to the groups to which the speakers *belong* –
a trade union in (38a) and a telecommunications company in (39a).

The Japanese 'system' of 'pronominals' looks rich in lexical variety, but this
means their selective employment depending on the context of speech events, but
not their pervasive use. As we have already seen in Chapter 3, the most prevailing alternative to the context-bound personal pronouns in Japanese is ellipsis.
Hinds argues that "ellipsis emerges as the principal means for indicating coreference" (1986a: 106–107), and that it is an unmarked indicator of topic continuity
(1983: 49). In English, by contrast, unstressed pronouns fulfill the same functions
(Fox 1987: 139). On top of the statistics presented in Chapter 3, several case studies numerically revealed the overwhelming dominance of ellipsis as a means of
person reference in Japanese. Martin (1975: 185), for instance, demonstrates that
grammatical subjects can undergo ellipsis as much as 74% of the time in daily

conversational interactions, and that as much as 37% of the time in expository writing. Shibamoto (1980) argues that object ellipsis is also very frequent in spoken Japanese and reports that as much as 67% of the objects of verbal predicates can be elliptical.

What is the 'elliptical mind-style' behind this extremely 'large-scale linguistic pattern' in Japanese then? It is largely constituted of the notion of 'nothingness'. Human entities are expressed by nothingness (ellipsis) or left 'unexpressed', where their identity is self-evident through the context. This could further mean that, if not necessary, the Japanese elliptical mind-style allows the native speakers of this language to go without encoding human entities; in other words, 'nothingness' is the *most* natural and unmarked means of person reference. Nothingness hardly causes FTAs, making a sharp contrast between the censurable, taboo-laden personal pronouns in this language, whose basic characteristics have just been observed. To value nothingness is obviously one of the most notable cultural and behavioural norms of the Japanese-speaking world, as clearly seen in many forms of art – such as the meaningful 'empty' space in traditional Japanese paintings, garden design and floral arrangements.

Another characteristic feature of Japanese person reference is that demonstratives and common noun phrases modified by demonstrative adjectives are used, where personal pronouns are expected from a Western linguistic point of view, and this elucidates how strongly the Japanese person system is influenced by the phenomenon of 'positionalisation of persons'. In Japanese, place deictic terms constitute yet another category of noun phrases, which substitutes the context-bound Japanese personal pronouns with a hint of taboo nature, along with ellipsis. It has been generally recognised in a wide variety of languages of European and Asian stocks (including Greek, Latin, Japanese, Mongolian and a fairly large number of both Germanic and Romance languages) that fairly close connections hold between third person pronouns and place deictic terms, and that demonstratives are the etymological source of third person pronouns (cf., for instance, Andō 1986; Diessel 1999; Levinson 1983; Lyons 1968 and 1977; Yamamoto 1992b and 1999).

Actually, as I have argued earlier, the Japanese third person pronouns, *kare* ('he') and *kanojo* ('she'), were originally place deictic terms with *ka-* meaning 'distant'. The original meaning of the second person personal pronoun *anata* was 'that direction' with the particle *a-* signifying a distal entity. In the case of Japanese, the historical 'diversion' of demonstratives into personal pronouns is the result of a deference strategy of encoding little animacy, agency, responsibility, etc. and hence making periphrastic person reference (Yamamoto 1999: 82).

As for the basic nature of place deixis, Levinson (1983: 62) argues that "probably most languages grammaticalize at least a distinction between proximal and distal, but many make much more elaborate distinctions". As Kamio (1987 and 1990) maintains in an account of his theory of 'territory of information', English

Table 3. Paradigm of Japanese place deictics (Yamamoto 1992a: 14)

ko-terms		*so*-terms		*a*-terms	
kore	'this one'	sore	'that one'	are	'that one'
kono	'(of) this'	sono	'(of) that'	ano	'(of) that'
koko	'here'	soko	'there'	asoko	'over there'
kochira	'this way/side'	sochira	'that way/side'	achira	'that way/side'
konna	'like this'	sonna	'like that'	anna	'like that'
kō	'in this way'	sō	'in that way'	ā	'in that way'

is a language which encodes only a 'bipartite' distinction in demonstratives (including adnominal ones) and deictic adverbs. This distinction is dependent on proximity to the speaker, as the proximal deictics *this* and *here* and the distal deictics *that* and *there* demonstrate.[15] However, being a more place deictically oriented language than English, Japanese makes a more complex, 'tripartite' distinction of place deixis using three kinds of stem-morphemes *ko*-, *so*- and *a*-; the *ko*-terms refer to something closer to the speaker, the *so*-terms to entities close to the addressee and the *a*-terms to entities close to neither (cf. Hinds 1986a: 266), although, as Coulmas (1982: 216–217) argues, not all cases fall neatly into this classification. The Japanese system of place deictic terms can be schematised as in Table 3.

In Table 3, it is assumed that the domain of English 'that' roughly embraces the scopes of both *so*-terms and *a*-terms in Japanese, and this is why the English translations of *so*-terms and *a*-terms are basically the same (Yamamoto 1992a: 14). *Kore*, *sore* and *are* are demonstrative pronouns, and *kono*, *sono* and *ano* are demonstrative adjectives. *Kochira*, *sochira* and *achira* are directional forms. Given the censurable nature of Japanese personal pronouns and the overwhelming effect of 'positionalisation of persons' on the Japanese ways of person reference, it is essential to note that the demonstrative pronouns *kochira*, *sochira* and *achira* can be used to refer to the first, second and third person respectively. They do not happen to appear in the Japanese-English parallel corpora, but are illustrated in the examples below (*atchi* in (40c) is a casual and shortened form of *achira*).

(40) a. *Kochira   wa   Yamamoto   desu.*
         This:side TOP Yamamoto COP.
         'This is (I am) Yamamoto'.

     b. *Sochira-san   no   go-tsugō   shidai desu.*
         That:side-HON GEN HON-convenience up:to COP.
         'It depends on your convenience'.

     c. *Atchi   wa   ki-ni-shi te nai mitai ne.*
         That:side TOP mind   to NEG seem COP.
         'He/she/they doesn't/don't seem to mind it'.

The demonstrative adjectives *kono* ('this'), *sono* ('that') and *ano* ('that') are often combined with a variety of common nouns that mean 'humans', such as *hito* ('person'), *kata* (polite and formal form of *hito*, originally meaning 'direction'), *yatsu* (a casual and rather stigmatised form roughly corresponding to the English word, 'guy') and *ko* ('child', 'boy' or 'girl'). The resulting forms, i.e. *kono hito, sono hito, ano hito, kono kata, sono kata, ano kata, koitsu, soitsu, aitsu* (the terms containing the word *yatsu* undergo the process of phonological reduction and become one word: e.g. *soitsu* = *so* + *yatsu*), *kono ko, sono ko, ano ko*, etc., function as 'pseudo personal pronouns' in Japanese (Yamamoto 1992a: 15). Those forms with *hito*, *kata* and *ko* are much 'safer', much less face threatening third person referential devices than personal pronouns. Unlike the cases of personal pronouns, the deictic nature of these terms does not entail strong 'inferred animacy', which embraces such factors as agency, intentionality and responsibility, since they characterise their referents in terms of very impersonal information, i.e. their spatial locations (Yamamoto 1999: 83).

The Japanese way of making person reference through place deictic terms can be closely associated with the metonymic person reference by means of place names as in *Nagoya wa kono ken ni-wa hantai rashii* ('Nagoya seems against this issue') (see Example (9) above), in that they both clearly reflect the particular mind-style shared by their native speakers that regards (or wishes to regard) human entities as 'places' or 'positions'. This impersonal 'positionalisation' world-view makes a very clear opposition to what was referred to as the English 'pronominal mind-style', that highlights the animate and personal aspects of human referents, which encapsulate their agency, responsibility, intentionality, etc.

The next subsection will address another issue where the English and Japanese mind-styles tend towards the opposite directions: it is a contrast between the individualistic and collectivistic views on the world – or that between individual- and collective-mindedness. The discussions will be biassed towards collectivism, with a special focus on notable socio-cultural phenomena as a means of characterising Japanese collectivistic values. According to the concept of 'cultural relativism' proposed by Franz Boas (1911), which originated from the awareness of different modes classifying the world and human experience in miscellaneous languages of America, the Japanese style of collectivism will not be interpreted as a part of what Boas referred to as the 'intellectually scaled master plan' in which 'familiar' languages and cultures of Europe occupy dominant positions (cf. Duranti 1997: 54).

4.4.2 Collectivism *vs.* individualism

The distinction between 'collectivism' and 'individualism' is the major dimension of cultural variability isolated by theorists across disciplines (cf. Gudykunst & San

Antonio 1993; Hofstede 1980; Itō 1989; Triandis 1988 and 1990). Naturally, individualism can be associated with the importance of 'personal' issues, but, by contrast, collectivism can be regarded as inherently constituting one form of the 'impersonality' concept, in which the existence of individuals is not articulated. 'Individualistic' cultures emphasise the goals of the individual over group goals, whilst 'collectivistic' cultures stress group goals over individual goals, with individuals belonging to collectives or ingroups[16] which 'look after' them in exchange for each individual member's 'loyalty' (Gudykunst & San Antonio 1993:29).

Earlier in this chapter, the clear inclination of Japanese towards group/collective agency rather than individual human agency was witnessed through statistical data, and this makes a sharp contrast with the English way of articulating individual human agency. In the journalistic texts within the parallel Japanese/English corpora (i.e. Texts 3 and 4), there are 23 cases (out of the total 600), where English animate/individuated expressions correspond to Japanese collective (inanimate and unindividuated) expressions. One of the examples considered in Chapter 3 was the correspondence between 'the Clinton administration' (*Kurinton seiken* in Japanese) and 'President Clinton himself', which is repeated in (41) below:

(41)   a.   [*Kurinton seiken*   ga   mizukara   seoikon-da]   seiji
             [Clinton administration NOM voluntarily shoulder-PART] political
             kadai
             problem
                                              (Text 3: *Asahi Shimbun*, 20 September 1994)
       b.   a political problem [that President Clinton himself stepped forward to
             tackle in the first place]
             (Text 3: *Asahi Evening News* (the English translation of the above), 20
             September 1994)

On the one hand, the Japanese expression *Kurinton seiken* ('Clinton administration') in (41a) refers to an impersonal and abstract group agent *which* makes a collective decision and acts collectively. However, on the other hand, its corresponding expression *President Clinton himself* in (41b) encodes the highly personal agency and responsibility of Bill Clinton as an individual 'Agent', with the reflexive pronoun *himself* intensifying the sense of individuation.

Other examples from the parallel corpora, that we have examined in Section 4.2, included the use of such pronouns in Japanese as *uchi* ('(my/our) house') and *o-taku* ('(your) house'), as well as the oppositions between Japanese impersonal and collectivistic expressions and English personal and individualistic expressions such as: 'Keisatsu-chō' ('the National Police Agency') *vs.* 'the officers on a high echelon', 'Roshia-gawa' ('Russian side') *vs.* 'the Russians', Calvin Klein as a company *vs.* Calvin Klein as an individual designer, and so forth. In these instances, the same human entities are expressed as highly individuated, responsible agents in English, but, in Japanese, as impersonal constituents of groups and institutions or buried under the dominance of a faceless mass. All these contrasts seem to be closely intertwined with (or can be ascribed to) the opposition between the individualistic behavioural norms (and the individualistic world-view/mind-style) manifested in the English language and the collectivistic behavioural norms (and the collectivistic world-view/mind-style) manifested in the Japanese language.

Collectivistic and individualistic mind-styles and cultural norms can also be observed in a much simpler linguistic phenomenon than the articulation and obfuscation of agency. Consider the simple manners of identifying oneself in a business setting in Japanese- and English-speaking societies:

(42) a. Ø Tōkyō-Mitsubishi Ginkō no Koizumi desu.
          (I) Tokyo-Mitsubishi Bank LK Koizumi COP.
      b. I'm Peter Patterson at Barclays Bank, Bene't Street.

Almost without exceptions, a Japanese businessman informs his potential business partner or customer of his affiliation first – 'Tokyo-Mitsubishi Bank' in the case of (42a) – that precedes his personal identity. However, again almost without exceptions, a businessman in the English-speaking world refers to himself as an individual agent first, and this is followed by his affiliation, which is 'Barclays Bank, Bene't Street' in (42b) above.

This example of greeting serves as a very simple but clear illustration of collectivistic and individualistic mind-styles in everyday social life, but a little more complex and systematic manifestations of such values can be found as a form of 'prescriptive' codes in daily business settings. In the rest of this subsection, our focus will be upon Roger Goodman's (1993) study on the Japanese work ethic and on workers' and employers' socio-cultural norms, which are clearly outside the Western 'intellectually scaled master plan' and hence provide a strong case that supports the concept of (socio-)cultural relativism. An understanding of such cultural values may also help (in an indirect way) the readers rediscover the completely opposite, individualistic behavioural norms of the English-speaking world.

In the case of Japanese society, as Goodman (1993:76) argues, it is the big companies which provide the 'model of ideal workplace', because of the 'security' they can provide for their workers in terms of higher salaries, but, at the same time, they require their workers to be 'ideal workers'. The sense of 'security' here is an important factor which both leads to and stems from the Japanese collectivistic world-view, that regards group affiliation as one of the most significant aspects of life; there is even a proverb which goes: "*Yoraba taiju no kage*", meaning "Go to the shade of a big tree (if you want to be safe or protected)". Goodman's illustration of the ideal qualities that ideal Japanese companies demand of their employees is somewhat revealing when considering the stereotypical Japanese value/norm concerning a sense of human agency, which is impersonal and collectivistic. He observes that an ideal Japanese male worker is:

(43) a. a worker who will conform to the company ideology and not cause trouble;

   b. a worker who will work hard and put the company before his personal well-being;

   c. a worker who will persevere and always try his hardest and

   d. a worker who is literate, numerate, and has generally proved his ability in being able to understand and apply new ideas quickly when they are put to him.   (Goodman 1993:76)

Thus, to a considerable extent, companies can collectively control the behaviours and mentality of their (male) workers. Goodman's idea of an 'ideal female worker' is also as revealing as the above qualities required of male workers by their employers, although it seems to be the case that, as the number of women employed in the workplace (who will stay in their workplaces after their marriage) increased, the same conditions as postulated in (43) began to be demanded from female employees. (44) illustrates the images of the ideal female worker which Goodman characterises:

(44) a. a worker who will cheer up the workplace by her presence (the 'office flower');

   b. a worker who will leave when she gets married and become: a wife who provides a comfortable home for a husband to relax in after work and a mother who will ensure that her children become the ideal (male or female) workers of the next generation.   (Goodman 1993:76)

The impersonality concept and the accompanying collectivistic value in the Japanese-speaking community, that prompt the superiority of group agency over individual agency, are clearly reflected in the actual behavioural codes as described in (43) and (44).[17]

The images of 'ideal' male and female employees in (43) and (44) are widely held in Japanese society; essentially, Japanese company workers, including both blue-collar and white-collar workers, are regarded as owing his/her first allegiance to his/her employers. Particularly, "the ideal male worker is prepared to sublimate his individual desires and ideas to the whole company ethic" (Goodman 1993:76). It is obvious that the Japanese style of collectivism presupposes a sense of 'selflessness', which can naturally be associated with the 'elliptical mind-style' that I have explored in the previous subsection.

The contrast between the collectivistic *vs.* individualistic norms in Japanese- and English-speaking cultures represents an interesting case of socio-cultural relativity – relativity on the levels of 'culture' in terms of the three-layered structure of relativism as presented in Figure 2. Through observing the articulation and obfuscation of agency in English and Japanese or, under a different guise, the opposition between the concepts of 'agency' and 'impersonality', we have shed light upon the different mind-styles concerning the interpretation of human entities and the socio-cultural norms behind surface linguistic manifestations. The current chapter also re-examined the 'linguistic relativity principle' *a la* Benjamin Lee Whorf and introduced the neo-Whorfian way of interpreting the co-relation between language, thought and culture. At least, as far as the opposition between the Japanese and English ways of making person reference and encoding agency and impersonality are concerned, the relativistic views on 'language', 'thought' and 'culture' work and work well, with the traditional, original form of Whorfian ideas and 'neo-Whorfianism' making hardly any contradiction with each other.

In the following chapter, we will address some 'enigmas' that we have not fully explored in the preceding chapters. On the basis of our previous discussions on philosophical characterisation of 'agency', the Japanese and English ways of expressing and suppressing it and the relativistic views on 'language', 'thought' and 'culture', more insights into the further study on agency will be provided from a different walk such as rhetoric, as well as through comparative approaches to languages of different stocks – particularly those belonging to the Balto-Finnic/Balto-Slavic and Celtic families.

CHAPTER 5

Some enigmas concerning agency, impersonality and 'reality'

O Winter! bar thine adamantine doors:
The north is thine; there hast thou built thy dark
Deep-founded habitation. Shake not thy roofs,
Nor bend thy pillars with thine iron car.

(William Blake, "To Winter")

5.1 Contribution to linguistics and philosophy

This chapter is a 'waste-basket' in this book, but it also serves as a concluding chapter. To start with, I shall first review our achievements in the three main chapters.

Chapter 2 was an attempt to establish the conceptual and philosophical framework of 'agency'. Our starting point was Aristotle's discussion on the opposition between the primacy of 'object' and that of 'action' and this ancient thinker's insight contributed to our aim a great deal. The arguments by the modern philosophers, such as Davidson, Chisholm, Searle and Thalberg, also constitute a good part of the conceptual framework of agency that is adopted in this book, which roughly goes like this: the concept of 'agency' presupposes those of 'intentionality' and 'animacy'.

We then focussed upon the epistemological salience of the agency concept, referring to the hypothetical language of a Neanderthal man and examining the degree of contribution of agency towards the notion of 'mind-style'. The cognitive salience of agency means that, by manipulating the expression of agency, one can manipulate the way the others would think and act; we have demonstrated that agency can often be a politically influential notion in this sense. Lastly, we re-examined the relationship between the agency concept and that of 'animacy', which has always been closely associated with the former, exploring the conceptual framework of animacy in detail.

Chapter 3 was focussed on the linguistic application of the agency concept, particularly, in syntax and semantics. Firstly we have reviewed the terminological arguments by the Case Grammarians (Fillmore, Chafe, *et al.*) and the Functional linguists (such as Simon Dik), and it was demonstrated that the characterisation of agency by linguists has always had recourse to the scale of 'semantic roles'. The 'linguistic model' that was adopted here is the Functional Grammarians' definition of agency and semantic roles, which is congenial to our philosophical arguments in Chapter 2.

A clear-cut conclusion drawn from the case study of the Japanese and English parallel corpora in Chapter 3 is that, in Japanese, the agent of an action often dissolves in some measure into nothingness, whereas, the tendency to express who/what performs an action prevails in English. On the one hand, the dominant clause type in English is an 'actor-action form' which highlights human/animate entities as agents or 'Agents' in Dik's (1989) terms. However, on the other hand, Japanese prefers an 'event form' of clause construction, where the existence and actions of humans and animates tend to be 'submerged' in the 'whole course of an event'. The articulation of one's agency sometimes brings about a face threatening effect, because the attribution of agency often means 'accusation' or assignment of 'responsibility' (Davidson 1971). The concept of 'impersonality' was introduced in Chapter 3, in an attempt to explain a series of linguistic phenomena, where human agentive entities are expressed as impersonal in one way or another, mostly by means of periphrastic referential expressions. We directed particular attention to such 'impersonality' phenomena in Japanese – that are prototypically manifested in the form of 'locationalisation' or 'positionalisation of persons' and the overwhelming use of ellipsis as a means of person reference – and treated them as a 'large-scale grammatical feature' of this language.

Chapter 4 went well beyond the structural arguments by linguists and revealed the further implication of the opposition between the obfuscation and articulation of agency, in search for the semantic, pragmatic and socio-cultural motives facilitating the particular patterns of encoding agency in Japanese and English. The contrastive ways of treating human agency in these two languages were ascribed to the different 'mind-styles' or 'world-views' and further to the different cultural and behavioural norms. A special focus was placed on the suppression of agency in Japanese, and various means of impersonalising human entities were investigated from pragmatic and socio-cultural points of view.

After giving some remarks on the historical background of the so-called 'Sapir-Whorf hypothesis', we re-examined in detail Benjamin Lee Whorf's (1956) 'linguistic relativity principle', in comparison with its recent reincarnation, 'neo-Whorfianism' (Levinson 2003) embellished with colourful examples from the Tzeltal language. We then brought the theoretical discussions on linguistic and socio-cultural relativity into practice to explicate the distinctive styles of encoding agency in Japanese and English and some significant socio-cultural facts that clearly reflect the 'collectivistic' view on human agency in Japanese, as opposed to the highly 'individualistic' expression of agency in English.

5.2 Shake not thy roofs: A rhetorical enigma

As we have reviewed so far, throughout the course of this book, our interest has always been in the agency of human (or at least highly animate) entities. However, according to the poet, William Blake, the season winter "built his dark, deep-founded habitation" and "shakes his roofs", as in the above quotation from his poem, "To Winter".

Is the 'winter' in this case to be interpreted as a 'Force' in the terminology of Simon Dik rather than an 'Agent' because the entity in question – or it may not even be an 'entity' at all – is inanimate? Under normal circumstances, the answer would be 'yes'. But in the metaphysical world of Blake's poetry, created perhaps through his 'vision', the answer to the same question could also be 'no'. To the poet, *the* winter may well be an irregular but fully-fledged 'Agent'.

Blake continues as follows:

(1) *He hears me not*, but o'er the yawning deep
     Rides heavy; his storms are unchain'd, sheathed
     In ribbed steel; I dare not lift mine eyes,
     For *he hath rear'd his sceptre o'er the world.*

If the true referent of the third person pronouns in this stanza is unknown, the first and last clauses that are in italics here are to be naturally regarded as expressing intentional 'actions' performed by an animate Agent. However, in the poetic world of William Blake, the identity of *he* and *his* is of course the season 'winter', which is not only inanimate but also abstract, but we should not discount the empathy[1] behind the use of animate personal pronouns, with which the poet invests 'winter'. For Blake, *the* winter could have represented a particular human individual who was highly agentive.

Thus, one of the reasonable interpretations of this particular 'winter' is that *he* is a 'metaphoric agent' in the above lines. As I mentioned above, Blake expresses the metaphorical (inferred) animacy and agency of 'winter' through the use of (1) second and third person pronouns and (2) verbs of motion and sentiency, which will be explained later with reference to the notion of 'pathetic fallacy'. Firstly, in the first stanza quoted at the beginning of this chapter, the poet addresses 'winter' referring to it (or him) by means of second person personal/possessive pronouns, and, in the second stanza (see (1)), he uses third person personal and possessive pronouns to refer to the same abstract entity. The use of personal pronouns and second person reference are means of encoding a strong sense of animacy (Yamamoto 1999: 23–35) and hence that of agency.

Here, we cannot disregard a very basic question concerning the possible borderland between the real and the unreal, which is most prototypically manifested as 'fiction' of some sorts. The philosopher John Searle argues that existence in the 'normal real world' and existence in fiction can be clearly distinguished from each other, and that referential expressions are concerned with either the normal real world or the fictional world (1969: Ch. 4). He further maintains that there is a clear-cut boundary between what he refers to as 'serious' discourse which deals with the normal real world and 'fictional' discourse which, needless to say, deals with the fictional world (Searle 1979: 70). However, cats *who* can read human mind (cf. Roger Caras' novel quoted in Chapter 1) might seem to be real to some people (including myself!), but they might be more or less 'fictional' to others (Yamamoto 1999: 13). As we observed in Chapter 2, Aristotle assumed that gods constitute a vital, unmissible part of his hierarchy of *psuchai*, and one cannot simply dismiss his opinion saying that gods belong to the realm of 'fiction'. For billions of people in the 'normal real world', the 'normal real world' without gods is just unthinkable.

Searle's idea of the clear borderline between reality and fiction seems to be based on a widely held common sense that normal human cognition must always be logical, and that normal human reason must always be reasonable. Indeed, however, 'real' human 'reason' can sometimes be utterly 'unreasonable'. Accordingly, as John Lyons (1977: 183) suggests, we must allow for various 'kinds' or 'modes' of existence, some of which might seem to be completely fictional in most cases – such as the agentive 'winter' in William Blake's above-mentioned poem (cf. Yamamoto 1999: 14).

In many cases, 'personification' entails authors' 'empathy', and so it is often identified as what literary critics call 'pathetic fallacy'. As Leech and Short (1981: 198) argue, 'pathetic fallacy' is a strong current in literary expression, although it is "evident deviation from a commonsense view of things", that is, under a different guise, deviation from 'serious discourse' concerning the 'normal real world'. Pathetic fallacy is typically manifested in the combination of inanimate entities with verbs of motion or sentiency (Leech & Short 1981: 198–199; Yamamoto 1999: 23), as can be exemplified in the expressions in the poem "To Winter": "there hast thou *built* thy dark/Deep-founded habitation", "He *hears* me not", "*Shake* not thy roofs", etc.

In the case of Blake's 'winter', the personifying metaphors may well be labelled as 'fallacy' of some measures, according to the definition of the term pathetic fallacy given above. However, when talking about the supernatural and deities, it can be ontologically biassed for one to regard gods' agency as 'fallacious'. Gods in such a case should be safely classified as 'supernaturally agentive', whilst the season 'winter' in Blake's poem is 'metaphorically agentive', and at the same time, they are also 'supernaturally animate' and 'metaphorically animate'. After all, 'agency', as well as 'animacy' on which the conceptual definition of 'agency' hinges, is a matter of degree or gradience and depends heavily on the epistemic attitudes of the observers of those entities in question. Indeed, we may have to allow for a variety of different kinds of agency, despite the syntactic rigour that we have adhered to since Chapter 3.

Considering another example illustrating a case of a pseudo figure of speech may be useful here. Such a passage as in (2) – that we considered in Chapter 3 – is not to be regarded as 'fallacious' in any senses, although it certainly carries a delicate but rather mundane metaphorical flavour:

(2)   The sleeveless shifts women are wearing this summer *stepped right out of the Onassis years*.   (Text 4: *Newsweek*, 29 August 1994)

The main clause of this extract provokes a major stylistic interest. As has been argued in Chapter 3, the italicised verb phrase *stepped right out of the Onassis years* gives the whole sentence a certain effect of personification, since it describes a state of affairs which is both [+ dynamic] and [+ control] in the terminology of Functional Grammar. In this sense, the subject is most likely to be a grammatical Agent, but can one really claim that the sleeveless shifts here are 'metaphorically agentive' as in the case of William Blake's 'winter'? The answer seems 'no': the *sleeveless shifts* are better interpreted as a kind of 'Force' in Dik's sense – or more precisely, a 'metaphorical Force'. The personification in this passage does not seem to involve much empathy of the writer towards the clothes and thus does not go so far as to cause pathetic fallacy, that we can characterise as a stronger and more rhetorically-oriented form of personification.

As we have argued throughout the course of this book, the actor-action pattern of clause formation is overwhelmingly prevalent in English. Personification often arises on the basis of the clear contrast between 'actor' and 'action', and an inanimate or an abstract noun phrase can be placed at the 'actor' position in a clause which is most prototypically occupied by a noun phrase referring to (or denoting) a human Agent (Ikegami 1991: 313). This is how even the inanimate and the abstract can be readily expressed as if they were syntactic agents through figurative use of language. Indeed, even 'pity' can 'cry' in this language.

Conversely, in Japanese, impersonal expression of events prevails and is commonly regarded as desirable, and 'personification' is sometimes viewed quite unfavourably as a means of figurative speech in the tradition of Japanese literature (Ikegami 1982 and 1991). For instance, the English Japanologist, Basil Hall Chamberlain (1939) observed as follows:

(3)   Another negative quality (of Japanese) is the habitual avoidance of personification – a characteristic so deep-seated and all-pervading as to interfere even with the use of neuter nouns in combination with transitive verbs. Thus this language rejects such expressions as "the heat makes me feel languid," "despair drove him to commit suicide," ... etc.

Chamberlain's observations of 'things Japanese' (which is the title of his book) tend to be rather negative, and, to him, the lack of personification in the Japanese language was another of the things he did not like about the country and its culture.

Conversely, the Japanese novelist, Sōseki Natsume, exclaimed that the English ways of personifying abstract entities 'nauseated' him, bitterly criticising the lines like the following (1906: 355):

(4)   Gigantic Pride, pale Terror, gloomy Care,
       And mad Ambition shall attend her there:
       There purple Vengeance bathed in gore retires,
       Her weapons blunted, and extinct her fires:
       There hateful Envy her own snakes shall feel,
       And Persecution mourn her broken wheel:
       There Faction roar, Rebellion bite her chain,
       And grasping Furies thirst for blood, in vain.

(Alexander Pope, *Windsor Forest*)

However, at the same time, Natsume (1906: 345) observed that the personification of more concrete entities can sound fairly successful; such 'successful' examples include the following lines from Thomas Hardy's *Tess of the d'Urbervilles*: "The fire in the grate looked impish – demonically funny, as if it did not care in the least about her strait. The fender grimmed [*sic*] idly, as if it too did not care. The light from the water-bottle was merely engaged in a chromatic problem".

The general rhetorical 'norm' (or tendency) of refraining from personification in Japanese seems a natural result of its preference of the 'event' pattern of clause formation over the 'actor-action' pattern. As Levinson (2003: 306) maintains, it is noticeable how the mastery of grammatical and semantic distinctions in a certain natural language leads to specific rhetorical style which makes full use of particular parameters – i.e. particular patternings of describing events and actions – and downplays descriptive material that does not easily fit with the prevalent manners of dissecting the outside world. Different epistemic attitudes and different propensities towards personification/pathetic fallacy in certain natural languages clearly mirror different mind-styles or world-views of their native speakers.

In the overwhelming majority of cases, personification and 'pathetic fallacy' are supposed better to be avoided, according to the rhetorical norm in the Japanese language. However, in reality, the question on the acceptability of the rhetoric figure of personification in Japanese (as compared with that in English) may not be always as crystal clear as argued above. Here, we must allow for some space for individual 'tastes' which may from time to time breach the general stylistic norm – even in as collectivistic a linguistic community as Japan.

In Chapter 3, we have mentioned the influence of translational literature from Western languages on Modern Japanese after the late 19th century, including the use of personifying metaphors, with reference to the notion of 'translationese' whose examples abound in Text 2 of the parallel corpus. Therefore, it seems particularly rewarding to look into the masterpieces of ancient and medieval Japanese literature long before Western influence, where, unwittingly, one can find such poetic expressions as "clouds running fast", "leaves whispering", etc., that Natsume (1906:345) thought reminiscent of the above passage from *Tess of the d'Urbervilles*.

The ancient verses we will consider below are taken from the *Hyaku-nin Isshu*, or "Single Verses by a Hundred People", which were collected together in A.D. 1235 by Sadaie Fujiwara, who included as his own contribution verse No. 97. The poems are placed in approximately chronological order, and range from about the year 670 A.D. to the year of compilation (Porter 1909:iii). Japanese poetry has no rhyme or alliteration and little, if any, rhythm. All the verses in the *Hyaku-nin Isshu* Collection are what are termed as *tanka*s (meaning 'short songs') and have 5 lines and 31 syllables, arranged thus: 5-7-5-7-7. The verses in (5) and (7) below are original Japanese 'songs', and their English translations are found in (6) and (8). The translator, William Porter, adopted for the translation a five-lined verse of 8-6-8-6-6 metre, with the second, fourth and fifth lines rhyming.

In most cases, the Japanese original poems tend to suppress the agency of any entities being mentioned, let alone the inanimates, whereas their English translations by Porter tend to overtly manifest the obfuscated agency in the original pieces. This is clearly demonstrated in the pair of the original and translational poems in (5) and (6):

(5) *Oku   yama   ni*
      Deep mountain in

      Momiji   fumi-wake
      Maple:leaves tramp:PART

      Naku   shika   no
      Call:PART stag/deer GEN

      Koe kiku   toki zo
      Voice hearing time at

      Aki   wa kanashiki.
      Autumn TOP sad:COP.

                           (Original poem written by Saru Maru Tayū)

(6) I hear the stag's pathetic call
     Far up the mountain side,
     While tramping o'er the maple leaves

Wind-scattered far and wide
This sad, sad autumn tide.

This poem is verse No. 5 of "Single Verses by a Hundred People" and was written at a fairly early stage of medieval Japan. Very little is known of this poet, but he probably lived not later than A.D. 800.

As expressed in the English translation in (6), it is 'I' – i.e. the poet himself – who 'hears' the stag's pathetic call, and as 'hearing' is not usually classified as an intentional action, it is most likely that 'I' would be labelled as an 'experiencer', rather than an 'agent'. However, this same entity could also be interpreted as an 'agent' in that (1) the poet is clearly aware of what he is doing, and that (2) his act of 'hearing' involves his concentrated attention on the sad 'voice' of the stag and his emotional identification with the stag itself (or himself). In the original Japanese verse, the existence of the experiencer or the agent is not verbally expressed but constitutes a small part of the whole autumnal landscape of tranquillity, whereas, of course, Porter had to add the flavour of human intervention in translating this verse, which is otherwise untranslatable.

The verse in (7), which was written in the 9th century, is quite exceptional in the sense that it illustrates a good example of personification – perhaps as strong as to be referred to as 'pathetic fallacy':

(7) *Yama   gawa   ni*
    Mountain stream in

    Kaze   no   kake-taru
    Wind   NOM   build-PART

    Shigarami   wa
    Barrage   TOP

    Nagare   mo-ae-nu
    Flow   can-NEG:PART

    Momiji   nari-keri
    Maple:leaves   COP
        (Original poem written by Tsuraki Harumichi or Harumichi no Tsuraki)

(8) The stormy winds of yesterday
     The maple branches shook;
     And see! a mass of crimson leaves
     Has lodged within that nook,
     And choked the mountain brook.

The 'metaphorical force' or 'metaphorical agent' (or something in-between) encapsulated in the Japanese original poem is the wind building a barrage over a little mountain brook, which can readily be classified as an example of 'natural agents'.[2]

It must also be noted that the English translation in (8) contains two 'metaphor-ical forces' or 'metaphorical agents': (1) the 'stormy winds' that shook the maple branches and (2) a mass of crimson leaves choking the mountain brook, which, in the Japanese original, is only a motionless part of the entire picture and is not as prominently expressed as in the translational version.

5.3 Treatment of 'impersonal' constructions

Figurative speech is one of the areas which our arguments in Chapters 2–4 did not cover, but it is not the only enigma still to be explored. Another important issue in this 'waste-basket' chapter is the prospect of a more universal approach to 'impersonality' as the reverse of agency; in what follows, we will have a glimpse of the impersonal constructions in Estonian, Finnish and Irish, which are more neatly structured than what are found in Japanese.

The term 'impersonality' has been used in quite an abstract (and pretheo-retical) sense in the present work, designating various linguistic phenomena that suppress/obfuscate the sense of human agency in Japanese, including ellipsis, im-personal 'event-like' construction of a clause, 'positionalisation of persons', etc. However, it must be recognised here that, as I argued in Section 2.4, obfuscating agency as a means of rhetoric is not a 'patent' of the Japanese language, and that there are widely observed grammatical constructions labelled as 'impersonals' in a variety of languages in the world, that have sometimes been confused with rather peripheral variants of 'passives'. But "passive and impersonal constructions have a strikingly different status in current theoretical and descriptive studies" (Blevins 2003:1).

As Blevins (2003:1–45) argues, the languages which most characteristically manifest such impersonal constructions are those belonging to the Balto-Finnic and Balto-Slavic stocks and some members of the Celtic family. Unlike our loosely cognitive notion of 'impersonality' or 'impersonalness', which served to highlight the contrastive mind-styles reflected in the Japanese and English ways of mani-festing human agency, Blevins' definition of 'impersonals' is purely syntactic. He argues that impersonalisation uniformly defines a subjectless form, irrespective of the argument structure of its input, and that impersonalisation preserves tran-sitivity, merely inhibiting the syntactic realisation of a surface subject (Blevins 2003:3 and 9). As far as transitivity is concerned, one of the major differences between 'impersonals' and passives is that impersonal forms of transitive verbs retain grammatical objects.

Along with subjectlessness, what characterises impersonals is their association with indefinite, canonically human, agents, which are not verbally expressed; the constructions that will be examined below are dubbed as 'impersonals' in the sense

that (1) they obfuscate human agency by suppressing surface grammatical subjects, and that (2) they encode the flavour of indefiniteness or anonymity. The
examples we will examine below are taken from Estonian, Finnish and Irish, and
in all these instances indefiniteness plays an important role, unlike the cases we
have observed so far through the Japanese-English parallel corpora.

An impersonal 'voice' is a distinctive feature of Balto-Finnic (Blevins 2003:11),
and "in Estonian, 'voice' refers to whether the subject or agent of an action is
known or unknown" (Mürk 1997:21). According to Erelt *et al.* (1995), there is
a basic distinction in this language between 'personal verb forms' and 'impersonal
verb forms', which exist for each tense/mood/aspect combination, and impersonal
forms can be characterised as implying the involvement of an indefinite animate
subject which remains unspecified (cf. Erelt *et al.* 1995:73; Blevins 2003:11). In the
examples below, Erelt *et al.* illustrate this opposition by contrasting the personal
form *kaklesid* in (9a) with its impersonal counterpart *kakeldi* in (9b):

(9) a. *Poisid kaklesid   õues.*
         Boys   fight:PAST:3PL outside
         'The boys were fighting outside'.
     b. *Õues   kakeldi.*
         Outside   fight:PAST:IMP
         'People were fighting outside'.   (Erelt *et al.* 1995:73)

The implied or suppressed subjects accompanying impersonal verbs in Estonian are normally identified as human and not merely animate, and, in this sense,
they can be interpreted as semantically corresponding to the indefinite personal
pronouns – such as 'one' and 'man' in English, *man* in German and *on* in French
(cf. Blevins 2003:12). The sentence in (10a) below, which contains an impersonal
form of *haukuma* ('to bark'), cannot be interpreted as concerned with a dog, but
only with humans (Torn 2002:95), and it is to be regarded as containing figurative speech. Example (10b) is unacceptable, since inanimate verbs like *aeguma*
('to expire') cannot be combined with indefinite (and suppressed) human entities, and, as Blevins (2003:12) points out, it cannot be assigned a metaphorical
interpretation, either.

(10) a. *Õues   haugutakse.*
          Outside   bark:PRES:IMP
          'One barks outside'.   (Torn 2002:95)
      b. **Aegutakse/aeguti.*
          Expire:PRES:IMP/PAST:IMP
          'One expires/expired'.

In Finnish, too, the use of the impersonal form to suppress the syntactic realisation of an animate/human subject is of significant importance. Abondolo

(1998:171) states: "There is also a subparadigm of impersonal inflection, used when the subject is unknown, or to avoid stating the subject". As in Estonian, the impersonal can be formed from both intransitive and transitive verbs (Sulkala & Karjalainen 1992:288), provided that they can be combined with human or animate agents[3] (Blevins 2003:15). Consider the following example:

(11)   a.   *Talo   tuhottin.*
            House:NOM   destroy:PAST:IMP
            'The house was destroyed (by somebody or some people)'.
       b.   *Suomessa   ollaan   niin totisia.*
            In:Finland   be:IMP:PRES   so   serious:NOM:PL
            'In Finland, we/they/people are so serious'.   (cf. Shore 1988:159)

In neither (11a) nor (11b), human agency is verbally expressed. Commenting on the example (11a), Shore (1988:159) argues that "the Agent responsible for the process is human; the indefinite would not be used if the house were destroyed in a bushfire or in a cyclone". In (11b), the impersonal form of the verb *olla* indicates that unaccusatives which can be combined with human subjects can be freely impersonalised (Blevins 2003:15).

In the Celtic languages, such as Breton, Welsh and Irish, there is a process reminiscent of the 'impersonalisation' in the languages belonging to the Balto-Finnic and Balto-Slavic families, although the Celtic equivalents of impersonal verbs are often termed as 'autonomous' verb forms. As Fife (1993:15) argues, "basically, all Celtic languages possess an impersonal form for each tense which is neutral as to the person and number features of the subject". As in the cases of Estonian and Finnish, the Celtic autonomous constructions pattern syntactically with active clauses (Blevins 2003:29), and, in particular, autonomous forms of transitive verbs retain objects.

The Celtic 'autonomous impersonals' can also be defined in terms of subject-lessness; in Irish, for instance, the 'autonomous' form of a verb expresses only 'verbal' actions, without any mention of nominal entities that are agents or of any indication of person or number[4] (Christian Brothers 1990:94). As the Irish examples in (12) (Noonan 1994:288–289) illustrate, the anonymity of suppressed (agentive) subjects is another of their defining characteristics:

(12)   a.   *Bhíothas ag bualadh Thomáis.*
            Was:IMP   at hit:PROG Thomas:GEN
            'One/Someone was hitting Thomas'.
       b.   *Táthar cairdiúil anseo.*
            Is:IMP   friendly here
            'They/People are friendly here'.

The examples from Estonian, Finnish and Irish we considered above illustrate clearly structured manifestations of impersonality in terms of both grammatical rules and their conceptual basis. One of our most important and fruitful future tasks would be to establish a comprehensive perspective of impersonality or impersonalness which ideally accommodates not only the structurally clear cases, but also more cognitively-oriented cases of impersonality as has been observed in Japanese. Such a wider framework would hopefully enable us to explicate systematically various facets of impersonality – from its rigorously syntactic aspects to its hazily and complexly pragmatic and socio-cultural aspects.

Exploring 'local[5] parameters' concerning the manifestation of impersonality on various linguistic (and non-linguistic) levels and in a variety of languages of different stocks will, without doubt, contribute towards revealing a wide range of 'local flavours' of agency and impersonality in natural languages on the globe. For instance, 'anonymity' is a local parameter that is highlighted in Balto-Finnic, Balto-Slavic and Celtic languages, but is downplayed in Japanese and English. Impersonalisation of human entities through 'positionalisation of persons' is another local parameter, which is particularly salient in Japanese, but is not prevalent in English, Estonian, Finnish and Irish.

5.4 A neverending story

In bringing this book to a close, let us remind ourselves of Albert Einstein's famous remark that we considered at the beginning of Chapter 4: "… a paradox, namely that reality, as we know it, is exclusively composed of 'fancies.'"

All in all, every argument on agency and impersonality in this book has been concerned with the different fashions of dissecting 'reality' – if there is any – or with a variety of 'local' world-views. If what we call 'reality' were made up of 'fancies' of some measures as Einstein suspected, then another of our rewarding future tasks would be to explore different varieties of 'fancies' built in different varieties of mind-styles that populate this world. Also, there must be many other enigmas concerning agency and impersonality alongside rhetorical issues and the comprehensive treatment of impersonalisation in world languages, and so there still seems to be a long way to go to explore these topics.

It was in 1972 when the philosopher, Irving Thalberg, published his celebrated book, *Enigmas of Agency*. It is not certain whether Thalberg expected that we would be engaged in exactly the same concerns as his after thirty-three years; however, what we know for certain is that our problem is as old as the hills, dating back to the depths of Greek antiquity. It is not surprising at all, therefore, that our species will continue to be concerned with agency for another couple of millennia!

Notes

Chapter 1

1. However, it must be borne in mind that, in the field of linguistic anthropology, the relationship between language and world-view has always been a central concern, despite the unpopularity of the Sapir-Whorf hypothesis in the tradition of theoretical linguistics (Hill 1988; Koerner 1992; Duranti 1997).

2. Whorf preferred the expression 'principle' over the term 'hypothesis' that is pervasively used by later scholars (cf. Lee 1996).

Chapter 2

1. Davidson also argues, however, that agency is a simpler and more basic concept than intention (1971:8). In his article "Intending" (1978), he further maintains that 'pure' intending is to be treated as separate from the intended actions or the reasons that prompted the actions in question (2001:89).

2. Davidson also provides a similar case in another of his article on this topic, "Freedom to Act" (1973).

3. We should also note that Searle's capitalised 'Intentionality' is something quite different from the 'intentionality' notion in an ordinary sense. The capitalised Intentionality is a matter of direction and aboutness of mental states and events. "Intentionality is that property of many mental states and events by which they are directed at or about or of objects and states of affairs in the world" (1983:1), and "intending and intentions are just one form of Intentionality among others", such as belief, hope, fear, desire and so on (1983:3).

4. For more detailed discussions on Aristotle's account of this tragedy, see Barnes (1995) "Rhetoric and Poetics", pp. 277–282.

5. The terms 'intention' (or 'intentionality') and 'volition' are often mixed up with each other in many literatures on actions and agency. The reason lies in the interpretation of the term *hekousion* used in *Nicomachean Ethics*, which can be translated as either 'intentional' or 'voluntary'. I will adopt the position of Charles who argues: "I will take 'intentional' to be the correct translation of this term when applied to actions and not Ross' 'voluntary'" (Charles 1984:61).

6. See the note above.

7. This is a translation of a passage from *De Anima*, which is cited in Barnes (2000:105–106) with slight modification.

8. Cf. (1) David Hume, *Treatise of Human Nature* (ed. L. A. Selby-Bigge), Oxford: OUP, 1888 and (2) David Hume, *Enquiry Concerning Human Understanding* (ed. C. W. Hendel), New York: Liberal Arts, 1955.

9. For Aristotle's account of responsibility, which is largely a matter of ethics for him, see Hutchinson (1995:208–210).

10. The distinction between 'event' and 'action' can sometimes be quite ambiguous. In philosophy, 'action' is usually classified as a subcategory of 'event' (cf. Aristotle, Davidson, Searle, etc.), but quite often, linguists are not aware of this tradition and regard 'action' as an independent and equally-ranked concept which is incompatible with that of 'event'. In this book, I will not dare to make a clear characterisation of these two concepts, leaving their relationship rather fuzzy-edged.

11. For further discussions, see Yamamoto (1999:75–76).

12. In Yamamoto (1999), I treated the concept of 'politeness' as one of the potential parameters; however, in the current project, I regard politeness (including deference) as a derivative resulting from the complicated interaction between the four parameters which are listed here and other socio-cultural factors outside the scope of the animacy concept. (For the precise distinction between politeness and deference, see Thomas 1995:Ch. 6.) Further, in the current context, I would prefer the term 'the Agency Scale' over 'the Participant/Semantic Role Scale', obviously because our main concern throughout this book is nothing but 'agency'. The characterisations of (A) the General Animacy Scale, (B) the Hierarchy of Persons and (C) the Individuation Scale are mostly based on my previous discussions on animacy, as presented in Yamamoto (1999), although minor modifications have been made.

13. It is interesting to realise that later philosophers such as John Locke had a much simpler view of what can be termed as the animacy hierarchy. In *Essay Concerning Human Understanding* (2nd ed., 1694), Locke argued that the identity of one animal or one plant ('vegetable' in his word) lies in maintaining one and the same life, whilst the identity of one person is maintained through one and the same consciousness (in addition to one and the same life). Locke's argument here demonstrates a much stronger sense of 'anthropocentricity' than Aristotle's view of the natural world.

14. For thorough discussions on the treatment of personal pronouns in terms of the Individuation Scale, see Yamamoto (1999:Chs. 3–4). Animate entities are far more likely to undergo pronominalisation. The statistical correlation between animacy and pronominalisation has been clearly demonstrated in Yamamoto (1999:95–125) and Dahl and Fraurud (1996:56–57).

Chapter 3

1. Concerning the 'localistic' views on clause construction, see also Anderson (1971 and 1977); Jackendoff (1972 and 1987).

2. Dahl (2000) argues that, in addition to animacy, what he refers to as 'egophoricity' is also deeply involved in the determination of agency. Egophoric reference is basically defined as reference to speech act participants and generic reference, and "as shown by adult conversational data from Swedish, English, and Spanish, and longitudinal data from one Swedish child, the majority of all animate arguments of verbs in conversation are egophoric" (2000:37). He further maintains that, in general, positions that are restricted to animate reference, i.e. arguments representing agents, experiencers and recipients, also have a high incidence of egophoric reference (Dahl 2000:71).

3. Davidson's (1971) view of agency avoids the specious (but popular) association of action with activity and undergoing with passivity. An undergoer's participation in an action, in contrast to an agent's, needs be neither conscious nor volitional. Klaiman (1991:113) argues: "That agency and undergoing have reality in structural organisation and comprise grammatically significant statuses is part of the lore of the Western grammatical tradition, particularly in the study of grammatical voice".

4. A similar distinction has been made by Monane and Rogers (1977) and Hinds (1986b) under the names of 'situation focus' and 'person focus'.

5. For the statistical data demonstrating the pervasiveness of ellipsis as a means of person reference, see Yamamoto (1999:95–126).

6. The terms 'zero anaphora', 'null anaphora' or 'gapping' refer to the same phenomenon which is called 'ellipsis' in this book. For a generative interpretation of ellipsis, see, for instance, Tsujimura (1996:212–215), although the transformational analysis of this phenomenon may not seem always convincing.

7. Japanese 'personal pronouns' behave in quite the same way as nouns do. They can be modified by determiners and relative clauses and embrace a wide range of lexical forms which are to be selected according to such contextual factors as the human relationship between speakers, addressees and referents. As for the peculiarity of the Japanese person system, particularly the characteristics of Japanese personal pronouns, see Yamamoto (1999:76–84) and Hinds (1975 and 1986a).

8. For the detailed definition of 'parallel corpus' and their variations, cf. Baker (1995).

9. The six types of texts here constitute a part of the corpora data which I have previously used for the statistical analysis in Yamamoto (1999).

10. The contrast between an 'event form' and an 'actor-action form' of clause construction may also be reminiscent of that between 'thetic' and 'categorical' judgements, which were proposed by Franz Brentano and Anton Marty and developed by Kuroda (1972), Sasse (1987) and others in connection with grammatical theories, although they are to be regarded as quite a different matter from our current interest. It is somewhat revealing that Kuroda (1972) does not recognise English as a typically categorically-oriented language (Yamamoto 1999:175).

11. The Agent of killing 83 people in the example (30) is the international terrorist, 'Carlos the Jackal', who has been mentioned earlier in this chapter.

12. This expression has been taken from Hinds (1975).

13. Whorf continues as follows:

> We have to say 'It flashed' or 'A light flashed', setting up an actor, 'it' or 'light', to perform what we call an action, "to flash". Yet the flashing and the light are one and the same! The Hopi language reports the flash with a simple verb, *rehpi*: 'flash (occurred)'.
>
> (Whorf 1956:243)

Whorf's interpretation of 'action' seems slightly different from our definition of the agency concept outlined in Chapter 2, and his argument here seems to be focussed upon inanimate force and is hence outside the scope of the grammatical discussion on Agents in Dik's (1989) terms. However, Whorf's insight contributes to a wider interpretation of the opposition between the articulation of agency in constructing a clause and the impersonal formation of a proposition, which will be one of the main themes in the following chapter. According to our argument in the current chapter, Japanese shares a certain degree of agentless interpretation of 'Events' of particular kinds with the Hopi language: for example, the Japanese translation of *It flashed* in English or *Rehpi* in Hopi is: *Hikat-ta*, meaning exactly 'flash (occurred)'.

14. As shown in Table 1 (and exemplified in (33) and (34) above), there are 8 cases where English Agents and Japanese inanimates correspond to each other. It can be argued that, as far as the correspondence of inanimate entities with animate Agents is concerned, the difference between Japanese and English does not seem to be highly significant, compared with that in the use of ellipsis.

15. For the reasons why personal pronouns cannot be employed frequently as an unmarked means of person reference in Japanese, see Hinds (1975), Yamamoto (1992a) and Yamamoto (1999: Ch. 3, pp. 76–84 *inter alia*).

Chapter 4

1. Cited from H. L. Samuel (1952) *Essay in Physics* (*with a letter from Dr. Albert Einstein*).

2. This expression refers to what is most frequently (and more popularly) referred to as 'the linguistic relativity hypothesis' or 'the Sapir-Whorf hypothesis'. However, the term 'the linguistic relativity principle' will be regarded as more favourable than its alternatives, because, as Penny Lee (1996: 84) argues, Whorf himself regarded his arguments not as constituting 'hypotheses' but as representing 'principles'.

3. It must be borne in mind, however, that these characteristic cases do not cover the whole story. There are also cases where, an English Agentive expression, that is, at the same time, the 'figure' of a clause, has its Japanese equivalent in the corpus, which is neither an Agent nor a 'figure', with a different noun phrase functioning as a figure – but without involving senses of localionalisation or group/institutionalised agency. What follows is one such instance but has not been included in the numerical data in Tables 1 and 2 in Chapter 3:

> a. *Shikamo* <u>*senmonka ni-yoreba*</u>, *Toresu no   jiken wa   hyōzan no   ikkaku*
>   Besides   <u>expert to-according</u>, Torres GEN case TOP iceberg GEN one:corner
>   *ni-sugi-nai.*
>   no:more:than-COP:NEG.
>
>   (Text 4: *Newsweek* (Japanese edition), 31 August 1994)
> b. And, if Torres and his associates could obtain …, <u>authorities</u> say, it was probable that
>   others could, too.   (Text 4: *Newsweek*, 29 August 1994)

On the one hand, the Japanese expression *senmonka* ('expert(s)') in (a) appears in a non-Agentive, 'satellite' position inside a postpositional phrase and is naturally a part of the 'ground' of this extract. However, on the other hand, its English counterpart in (b), *authorities*, is clearly both the Agent and figure in a parenthetical clause. The 'figure' in the Japanese translational text is *Toresu no jiken* ('the case of Torres'), which is an inanimate noun phrase and hence can never function as an Agent. Any entity in a clause can be either highlighted as its 'figure' or made obscure as a part of its 'ground'. When considering the diversity of 'mind-styles' which is reflected in a variety of natural languages, the propensity concerning what kind of nominal entities should be likely to function as a figure (and/or an Agent) seems to give us some vital clues to different styles of thinking in constructing a proposition.

4. Strictly speaking, the Japanese text in (11a) is not a fully-fledged clause, because it does not contain any proper verb phrase. The last word '*hitei*' is not a verb but a noun meaning 'denial'.

5. In seven cases, however, Japanese animate/individuated expressions correspond to English inanimate/unindividuated expressions.

6. This is extracted from his paper "Gestalt Technique of Stem Composition in Shawnee", which first appeared in C. F. Voegelin, *Shawnee Stems and the Jacob P. Dunn Miami Dictionary* (Indianapolis: Indiana Historical Society, 1940).

7. More precisely, however, relatively contemporary formulations of the linguistic relativity hypothesis date back to eighteenth-century Germany, with the works by Machaelis, Hamann and Herder. For more detailed discussions, see Lucy (1992a).

8. As stated earlier, Whorf himself never spoke of any 'hypothesis', preferring the term 'principle' (cf. Lee 1996:84–85).

9. Jane Hill (1988:15) further points out that Fishman (1982) has noted the importance of a 'Whorfianism of the third kind'. It is an 'ethical' linguistic relativism, which insists on the value of 'little languages' like Hopi as precious contributions to the totality of human cognitive potentiality. This concept seems quite close to that of 'cultural relativism' proposed by Franz Boas (1911) that was mentioned in Chapter 1.

10. However, it must be borne in mind that, in the field of linguistic anthropology, the relationship between 'language' and 'world-view' has always been a central concern, despite the unpopularity of the Sapir-Whorf hypothesis in the tradition of theoretical linguistics (Hill 1988; Koerner 1992; Duranti 1997).

11. This refers to a Hopi cultural institution involving announcing, or preparative publicity, which Whorf has discussed (cf. Lucy 1992a:66).

12. Of course, personal pronouns can also encode the relative social standings of the speakers, addressees and referents. The distinctive use of a variety of Japanese pronouns of different kinds will be discussed later. In Indo-European languages, how socially superior participants, socially inferior participants and socially equal participants address and refer to one another can be explained in terms of the criteria of 'power' and 'solidarity' and the use of 'T-type' second person pronouns and 'V-type' second person pronouns (Brown & Gilman 1960; Brown 1972).

13. Particularly, in the case of nicknames, different people may call the same individual by different nicknames. In fact, T. S. Eliot writes in his *Old Possum's Book of Practical Cats* that cats usually have more than four names!

14. The 'equality' mentioned here cannot be explained only in terms of the concept of 'solidarity' *a la* Brown and Gilman (1960 and 1972). The distinctive use of each pronoun is heavily dependent on the gender of the speaker and referent and the relative formality of (and the 'topics' in) the speech event in question.

15. However, if we take account of the domain of the term *yonder*, it can be argued that English used to make (or still makes) a 'tripartite' distinction of place (Yamamoto 1999:128).

16. The term 'ingroups' here means "groups of people about whose welfare one is concerned, with whom one is willing to cooperate without demanding equitable returns, and separation from whom leads to discomfort or even pain" (Triandis 1988:75).

17. Specific examples of the collectivistic norm in Japanese-speaking society include: Cole's (1971) study of Japanese blue-collar workers in a modern factory and Rohlen's (1974) ethnography of a Japanese bank focussed on traditional Japanese spiritual education in the training and integration of Japanese employees into a company (Gudykunst & San Antonio 1993).

Chapter 5

1. Perhaps, the most well-known definition of 'empathy' from a linguistic point of view was given by Kuno and Kaburaki (1977:628), who stated: "Empathy is the speaker's identification, with a person who participates in the event that he describes in a sentence". It is of course necessary to expand the scope of Kuno and Kaburaki's above definition, so that it can be applied not only to human entities but also to other animate and inanimate (sometimes abstract) entities, and that it can explain linguistic phenomena on a discourse level. For further discussions, see Langacker (1991:306) and Yamamoto (1999:10–11).

2. The 'winter' in William Blake's above-mentioned poem can also be characterised as a 'natural agent'.

3. Interestingly, Shore (1988:160) notes that extensions of impersonals in Finnish apply even to enzymes in biology texts.

4. For the characterisation of the autonomous in Breton, see Hewitt (2002:30). For the equivalent construction in Welsh, see Morris Jones (1955:316–317) and King (2003:224).

5. For more arguments on the concept of 'locality' here, see Slobin (2001).

References

Abondolo, D. (1998). Finnish. In Abondolo (Ed.) 1998.

Abondolo, D. (Ed.). (1998). *The Uralic Languages*. London: Routledge.

Alford, D. K. (1981). Is Whorf's relativity Einstein's relativity? *Proceedings of the Berkeley Linguistics Society, 7*, 13–26.

Anderson, J. M. (1971). *The Grammar of Case*. Cambridge: CUP.

Anderson, J. M. (1977). *On Case Grammar*. Atlantic Highlands, NJ: Humanities Press.

Anderson, S. R. & E. L. Keenan (1985). Deixis. In Shopen (Ed.) 1985.

Andō, S. (1986). *Eigo no Ronri, Nihongo no Ronri* (The Logic of English and the Logic of Japanese). Tokyo: Taishūkan.

Aristotle. *De Anima*.

Aristotle. *De Motu Animalium*.

Aristotle. *Eudemian Ethics*.

Aristotle. *Nicomachean Ethics*.

Bach, E. & R. Harms (Eds.). (1968). *Universals in Linguistic Theory*. New York, NY: Holt, Rinehart & Winston.

Baker, M. (1995). Corpora in translation studies: An overview and some suggestions for future research. *Target, 7* (2), 223–243.

Ball, M. J. & J. Fife (Eds.). (1993). *The Celtic Languages*. London: Routledge.

Barnes, J. (1995). Rhetoric and poetics. In Barnes (Ed.) 1995.

Barnes, J. (2000). *Aristotle: A very short introduction*. Oxford: OUP.

Barnes, J. (Ed.). (1995). *The Cambridge Companion to Aristotle*. Cambridge: CUP.

Berlin, B. & P. Kay (1969). *Basic Color Terms: Their universality and evolution*. Berkeley, CA: University of California Press.

Berman, J. (Ed.). (1990). *Nebraska Symposium on Motivation* (Vol. 37). Lincoln, NB: University of Nebraska Press.

Bickel, B. (1997). Spatial operations in deixis, cognition, and culture: Where to orient oneself in Belhare. In Nuyts and Pederson (Eds.) 1997.

Binkley, R., R. Bronaugh & A. Marras (Eds.). (1971). *Agent, Action, and Reason*. Oxford: Basil Blackwell.

Blevins, J. P. (2003). Passives and impersonals. *Journal of Linguistics, 39*, 1–48.

Bloomfield, L. (1933). *Language*. London: George Allen & Unwin.

Boas, F. (1911). Introduction. In Boas (Ed.), *Handbook of American Indian Languages* (Vol. BAE-B40, part I). Washington, DC: Smithsonian Institution.

Bowerman, M. & S. Levinson (Eds.). (2001). *Language Acquisition and Conceptual Development*. Cambridge: CUP.

Brown, G. & G. Yule (1983). *Discourse Analysis*. Cambridge: CUP.

Brown, P. (1994). The ins and ons of Tzeltal locative expressions: The semantics of static descriptions of location. *Linguistics, 32*, 743–790.

Brown, P. & S. C. Levinson (1978). Universals in language usage: Politeness phenomena. In Goody (Ed.) 1978.

Brown, P. & S. C. Levinson (1987). *Politeness: Some universals in language usage*. Cambridge: CUP.

Brown, R. (1972). *Psycholinguistics*. New York, NY: Free Press.

Brown, R. & A. Gilman (1960). The pronouns of power and solidarity. In Sebeok (Ed.) 1960.

Callon, M. (1986). Some elements of a sociology of translation: Domestication of the scallops and the fishermen of St. Brieux Bay. In Law (Ed.) 1986.

Caras, R. A. (1989). *A Cat is Watching*. London: Harper Collins.

Chafe, W. L. (1970). *Meaning and the Structure of Language*. Chicago, IL: The University of Chicago Press.

Chamberlain, B. H. (1939). *Things Japanese* (Sixth edition). London: Kegan Paul.

Charles, D. (1984). *Aristotle's Theory of Action*. London: Duckworth.

Chatman, S. (Ed.). (1971). *Literary Style: A symposium*. Oxford: OUP.

Chisholm, R. M. (1966). Freedom and action. In Lehrer (Ed.) 1966.

Christian Brothers, The (1990). *New Irish Grammar*. Dublin: CJ Fallon.

Christie, A. (1934). *Murder on the Orient Express*. London: Harper Collins.

Cole, R. (1971). *Japanese Blue Collar: The changing tradition*. Berkeley, CA: University of California Press.

Comrie, B. (1989). *Language Universals and Linguistic Typology* (Second edition). Oxford: Basil Blackwell.

Cook, W. A. (1989). *Case Grammar Theory*. Washington, DC: Georgetown University Press.

Coulmas, F. (1982). Some remarks on Japanese deictics. In Weissenborn & Klein (Eds.) 1982.

Croft, W. (1990). *Typology and Universals*. Cambridge: CUP.

Croft, W. (2003). *Typology and Universals* (Second edition). Cambridge: CUP.

Cruse, D. A. (1973). Some thoughts on agentivity. *Journal of Linguistics, 9*, 11–23.

Dahl, Ö. (2000). Egophoricity in discourse and syntax. *Functions of Language, 7* (1), 37–77.

Dahl, Ö. & K. Fraurud (1993). Animacy in grammar and discourse. A paper read at the *4th International Pragmatics Conference*, Kobe, Japan, 25–30 July 1993.

Dahl, Ö. & K. Fraurud (1996). Animacy in grammar and discourse. In Fretheim & Gundel (Eds.) 1996.

Davidson, D. (1971). Agency. In Binkley, Bronaugh & Marras (Eds.) 1971.

Davidson, D. (1973). Freedom to act. Reprinted in Davidson 2001.

Davidson, D. (1978). Intending. Reprinted in Davidson 2001.

Davidson, D. (1980). *Essays on Actions and Events*. Oxford: OUP.

Davidson, D. (2001). *Essays on Actions and Events* (Second edition). Oxford: OUP.

Diessel, H. (1999). *Demonstratives: Form, function and grammaticalization*. Amsterdam: John Benjamins.

Dik, S. C. (1978). *Functional Grammar*. Amsterdam: North-Holland.

Dik, S. C. (1989). *The Theory of Functional Grammar. Part I: The structure of the clause*. Dordrecht: Foris.

Dixon, R. M. W. (1979). Ergativity. *Language, 55*, 59–138.

Dixon, R. M. W. (1994). *Ergativity*. Cambridge: CUP.

Dixon, R. M. W. (Ed.). (1976). *Grammatical Categories in Australian Languages*. Canberra: Australian Institute of Aboriginal Studies.

Dowty, D. R. (1979). *Word Meaning and Montague Grammar: The semantics of verbs and times in generative grammar and Montague's PTQ*. Dordrecht: Reidel.

Dowty, D. R. (1991). Thematic proto-roles and argument selection. *Language, 67*, 547–619.

Duranti, A. (1997). *Linguistic Anthropology*. Cambridge: CUP.

Eliot, T. S. (1939). *Old Possum's Book of Practical Cats*. London: Faber & Faber.

Erelt, M., R. Kasik, H. Metslang, H. Rajandi, K. Ross, H. Saari, K. Tael & S. Vare (1995). *Eesti Keele Grammatika,* Vol. 1: *Morfoloogia*. Tallinn: Eesti Teaduste Akadeemia Eesti Keele Instituut.

Everson, S. (1995). Psychology. In Barnes (Ed.) 1995.

Fairclough, N. (1989). *Language and Power*. London: Longman.

Fife, J. (1993). Historical aspects: Introduction. In Ball & Fife (Eds.) 1993.

Fillmore, C. J. (1968). Case for case. In Bach & Harms (Eds.) 1968.

Fillmore, C. J. (1971). Some problems for Case Grammar. In O'Brien (Ed.) 1971.

Fishman, J. A. (1982). Whorfianism of the third kind: Ethnolinguistic diversity as a worldwide societal asset (The Whorfian hypothesis: Varieties of validation, confirmation, and disconfirmation II). *Language in Society, 11*, 1–14.

Flavell, J. H. & L. Ross (Eds.). (1981). *Social Cognitive Development*. Cambridge: CUP.

Foley, W. A. & R. D. Van Valin, Jr. (1984). *Functional Syntax and Universal Grammar*. Cambridge: CUP.

Foley, W. A. & R. D. Van Valin, Jr. (1985). Information packaging in the clause. In Shopen (Ed.) 1985.

Fowler, R. (1977). *Linguistics and the Novel*. London: Routledge.

Fox, B. A. (1987). *Discourse Structure and Anaphora*. Cambridge: CUP.

Fox, B. & P. J. Hopper (Eds.). (1994). *Voice: Form and function*. Amsterdam: John Benjamins.

Fretheim, T. & J. K. Gundel (Eds.). (1996). *Reference and Referent Accessibility*. Amsterdam: John Benjamins.

Fries, U., G. Tottie & P. Schneider (Eds.). (1994). *Creating and Using English Language Corpora*. Amsterdam: Rodopi.

Frith, C. D. (1992). *The Cognitive Neuropsychology of Schizophrenia*. Hove: Psychology Press.

Fuchs, C. & S. Robert (Eds.). (1999). *Language Diversity and Cognitive Representations*. Amsterdam: John Benjamins.

Gelman, R. & E. Spelke (1981). The development of thoughts about animate and inanimate objects: Implications for research on social cognition. In Flavell & Ross (Eds.) 1981.

Givón, T. (1984). *Syntax*. Amsterdam: John Benjamins.

Givón, T. (Ed.). (1983). *Topic Continuity in Discourse*. Amsterdam: John Benjamins.

Golding, W. (1955). *The Inheritors*. London: Faber & Faber.

Goodman, R. (1993). *Japan's 'International Youth': The emergence of a new class of schoolchildren*. Oxford: Clarendon Press.

Goody, E. N. (Ed.). (1978). *Questions and Politeness*. Cambridge: CUP.

Gruber, J. S. (1967). Look and see. *Language, 43*, 937–947.

Gudykunst, W. B. (Ed.). (1993). *Communication in Japan and the United States*. Albany, NY: State University of New York Press.

Gudykunst, W. B. & P. San Antonio (1993). Approaches to the study of communication in Japan and the United States. In Gudykunst (Ed.) 1993.

Gumperz, J. J. & S. C. Levinson (Eds.). (1996). *Rethinking Linguistic Relativity*. Cambridge: CUP.

Halliday, M. A. K. (1971). Linguistic function and literary style. In Chatman (Ed.) 1971.

Halliday, M. A. K. (1985). *An Introduction to Functional Grammar*. London: Edward Arnold.

Hallowell, A. (1958). Ojibwa metaphysics of being and the perception of persons. In Tagiuri & Petrullo (Eds.) 1958.

Hartmann, H. (1954). *Das Passiv*. Heidelberg: Winter.

Hewitt, S. (2002). The impersonal in Breton. *Journal of Celtic Languages, 7*, 1–39.

Hill, J. (1988). Language, culture, and world view. In Newmeyer (Ed.) 1988.

Hinds, J. (1975). Third person pronouns in Japanese. In Peng (Ed.) 1975.

Hinds, J. (1983). Topic continuity in Japanese. In Givón (Ed.) 1983.

Hinds, J. (1986a). *Japanese*. London: Croom Helm.

Hinds, J. (1986b). *Situation vs. Person Focus*. Tokyo: Kuroshio Shuppan.

Hinds, J. (Ed.). (1977). *Proceedings of the UH-HATJ Conference on Japanese Languages and Linguistics*. Honolulu, HI: University of Hawaii.

Hofstede, G. (1980). *Culture's Consequences*. Beverly Hills, CA: Sage.

Huddleston, R. D. (1970). Some remarks on Case Grammar. *Linguistic Inquiry, 1*, 501–511.

Hume, D. (1739). Of personal identity. In D. Hume, *Treatise of Human Nature*, Book I. Reprinted in Perry (Ed.) 1975.

Hume, D. (1955). *Enquiry Concerning Human Understanding* (edited by C. W. Hendel). New York, NY: Liberal Arts.

Hundt, M. (2004). Animacy, agentivity, and the spread of the progressive in Modern English. *English Language and Linguistics, 8* (1), 47–69.

Hutchinson, D. S. (1995). Ethics. In Barnes (Ed.) 1995.

Ikegami, Y. (1981). *'Suru' to 'Naru' no Gengogaku* (Linguistics of 'Doing' and 'Becoming'). Tokyo: Taishūkan.

Ikegami, Y. (1982). Hyōgen kōzō no hikaku (The comparison of the structures of expressions). In Kunihiro (Ed.) 1982.

Ikegami, Y. (1991). 'Do-language' and 'become-language': Two contrasting types of linguistic representation. In Ikegami (Ed.) 1991.

Ikegami, Y. (Ed.). (1991). *The Empire of Signs: Semiotic essays on Japanese culture*. Amsterdam: John Benjamins.

Itō, Y. (1989). Socio-cultural backgrounds of Japanese interpersonal communication style. *Civilisations, 39*, 101–137.

Jackendoff, R. (1972). *Semantic Interpretation in Generative Grammar*. Cambridge, MA: The MIT Press.

Jackendoff, R. (1987). The status of thematic relations in linguistic theory. *Linguistic Inquiry, 18*, 369–411.

Johansson, S. & K. Hofland (1994). Towards an English-Norwegian parallel corpus. In Fries, Tottie & Schneider (Eds.) 1994.

Johnson-Laird, P. N. & P. C. Wason (Eds.). (1977). *Thinking: Readings in cognitive science*. Cambridge: CUP.

Kamio, A. (1987). Proximal and Distal Information: A theory of territory of information in English and Japanese. PhD thesis, University of Tsukuba.

Kamio, A. (1990). *Jōhō no Nawabari Riron* (A Theory of Territory of Information). Tokyo: Taishūkan.

King, G. (2003). *Modern Welsh: A comprehensive grammar*. London: Routledge.

Klaiman, M. H. (1991). *Grammatical Voice*. Cambridge: CUP.

Koerner, E. F. K. (1992). The Sapir-Whorf hypothesis: A preliminary history and a bibliographical essay. *Journal of Linguistic Anthropology, 2* (2), 173–198.

Kunihiro, T. (Ed.). (1982). *Nichi-Eigo Hikaku Kōza*, Vol. 4: *Hassō to hyōgen* (Seminar in Japanese-English Contrastive Studies, Vol. 4: Inspiration and expression). Tokyo: Taishūkan.

Kuroda, S.-Y. (1972). The categorical and the thetic judgment. *Foundations of Language, 9*, 153–185.

Lakoff, G. (1987). *Women, Fire, and Dangerous Things: What categories reveal about the mind.* Chicago, IL: The University of Chicago Press.

Lakoff, G. & M. Johnson (1980). *Metaphors we Live by.* Chicago, IL: The University of Chicago Press.

Langacker, R. W. (1991). *Foundations of Cognitive Grammar,* Vol. 2: *Descriptive application.* Stanford, CA: Stanford University Press.

Law, J. (Ed.). (1986). *Power, Action and Belief: A new sociology of knowledge?* [Sociology Review Monograph]. London: Routledge & Kegan Paul.

Lee, P. (1996). *The Whorf Theory Complex: A critical reconstruction.* Amsterdam: John Benjamins.

Leech, G. N. (1981). *Semantics* (Second edition). Harmondsworth: Penguin.

Leech, G. N. & M. H. Short (1981). *Style in Fiction: A linguistic introduction to English fictional prose.* London: Longman.

Lehrer, K. (Ed.). (1966). *Freedom and Determinism.* New York, NY: Random House.

Levinson, S. C. (1983). *Pragmatics.* Cambridge: CUP.

Levinson, S. C. (1994). Vision, shape and linguistic description: Tzeltal body-part terminology and object description. *Linguistics, 32*, 791–855.

Levinson, S. C. (1996). Relativity in spatial conception and description. In Gumperz & Levinson (Eds.) 1996.

Levinson, S. C. (1997). From outer to inner space: Linguistic categories and non-linguistic thinking. In Nuyts & Pederson (Eds.) 1997.

Levinson, S. C. (2003). *Space in Language and Cognition: Explorations in cognitive diversity.* Cambridge: CUP.

Locke, J. (1694). Of identity and diversity. In Locke, *Essay Concerning Human Understanding* (Second edition). Reprinted in Perry (Ed.) 1975.

Longacre, R. E. (1956). Review of *Language and Reality* by Wilbur M. Urban and *Four Articles on Metalinguistics* by Benjamin Lee Whorf. *Language, 32*, 298–308.

Lucy, J. A. (1992a). *Language Diversity and Thought: A reformation of the linguistic relativity hypothesis.* Cambridge: CUP.

Lucy, J. A. (1992b). *Grammatical Categories and Cognition: A case study of the linguistic relativity hypothesis.* Cambridge: CUP.

Lucy, J. A. (1996). The scope of linguistic relativity: An analysis and review of empirical research. In Gumperz & Levinson (Eds.) 1996.

Lyons, J. (1968). *Introduction to Theoretical Linguistics.* Cambridge: CUP.

Lyons, J. (1977). *Semantics,* 2 Vols. Cambridge: CUP.

McLendon, S. (1978). Ergativity, case and transitivity in Eastern Pomo. *International Journal of American Linguistics, 44*, 1–9.

Malotki, E. (1979). *Hopi-Raum.* Tübingen: Narr.

Malotki, E. (1983). *Hopi Time: A linguistic analysis of the temporal categories in the Hopi language.* Berlin: Mouton.

Martin, S. E. (1975). *A Reference Grammar of Japanese.* New Haven, CT: Yale University Press.

Miller, G. & P. N. Johnson-Laird (1976). *Language and Perception.* Cambridge: CUP.

Minoura, Y. (1991). *Kodomo no Ibunka Taiken* (Cross-cultural Experience of Children). Tokyo: Shisaku-sha.

Mishima, Y. (1966). *Death in Midsummer and Other Stories.* Harmondsworth: Penguin.

Monane, T. & L. Rogers (1977). Cognitive features of Japanese language and culture and their implications for language teaching. In Hinds (Ed.) 1977.

Morris Jones, J. (1955). *A Welsh Grammar, Historical and Comparative: Phonology and accidence*. Oxford: Clarendon Press.

Mühlhäusler, P. & R. Harré (1990). *Pronouns and People*. Oxford: Basil Blackwell.

Mürk, H. W. (1997). *A Handbook of Estonian: Nouns, adjectives and verbs* [Indiana University Uralic and Altaic Series 163]. Bloomington, IN: Indiana University.

Myhill, J. (1992). *Typological Discourse Analysis*. Oxford: Basil Blackwell.

Natsume, S. (1906). *Bungaku-ron* (Treatise on Literature). Tokyo: Ōkura Shoten.

Newmeyer, F. J. (Ed.). (1988). *Linguistics: The Cambridge survey*, Vol. 4: *Language: The socio-cultural context*. Cambridge: CUP.

Nichols, J. & A. C. Woodbury (Eds.). (1985). *Grammar Inside and Outside the Clause: Some approaches to theory from the field*. Cambridge: CUP.

Noonan, M. (1994). A tale of two passives in Irish. In Fox & Hopper (Eds.) 1994.

Nuyts, J. & E. Pederson (Eds.). (1997). *Language and Conceptualization*. Cambridge: CUP.

O'Brien, R. J. (Ed.). (1971). *Report of the Twenty-second Annual Round Table Meeting on Linguistics and Language Studies*. Washington, DC: Georgetown University Press.

Pachoud, B. (1999). Schizophasia and cognitive dysfunction. In Fuchs & Robert (Eds.) 1999.

Palmer, F. R. (1981). *Semantics* (Second edition). Cambridge: CUP.

Palmer, F. R. (1994). *Grammatical Roles and Relations*. Cambridge: CUP.

Peng, F. C. C. (Ed.). (1975). *Language in Japanese Society*. Tokyo: University of Tokyo Press.

Perry, J. (Ed.). (1975). *Personal Identity*. Berkeley, CA: University of California Press.

Piaget, J. (1955). *The Language and Thought of the Child*. New York, NY: World. (Original work published in 1926.)

Piaget, J. (1969). *The Child's Conception of the World*. Totowa, NJ: Littlefield, Adams. (Original work published in 1929.)

Pick, H. L. & L. P. Acredolo (Eds.). (1983). *Spatial Orientation: Theory, research, and application*. New York, NY: Plenum.

Pickering, A. (Ed.). (1992). *Science as Practice and Culture*. Chicago, IL: The University of Chicago Press.

Porter, W. N. (1909). *A Hundred Verses from Old Japan: A translation of the Hyaku-nin-isshu*. Oxford: The Clarendon Press.

Primus, B. (1999). *Case and Thematic Roles: Ergative, accusative, active*. Tübingen: Niemeyer.

Pullum, G. (1991). *The Great Eskimo Vocabulary Hoax and Other Irrelevant Essays on the Study of Language*. Chicago, IL: The University of Chicago Press.

Quirk, R., S. Greenbaum, G. Leech & J. Svartvik (1985). *A Comprehensive Grammar of the English Language*. London: Longman.

Rohlen, T. P. (1974). *For Harmony and Strength*. Berkeley, CA: University of California Press.

Rosch, E. (1977). Linguistic relativity. In Johnson-Laird & Wason (Eds.) 1977.

Samuel, H. L. (1952). *Essay in Physics* (*with a letter from Dr. Albert Einstein*). New York, NY: Harcourt, Brace.

Sasse, H. (1987). The thetic/categorical distinction revisited. *Linguistics, 25*, 511–580.

Schlesinger, I. M. (1995). *Cognitive Space and Linguistic Case: Semantic and syntactic categories in English*. Cambridge: CUP.

Searle, J. R. (1969). *Speech Acts*. Cambridge: CUP.

Searle, J. R. (1979). *Expression and Meaning*. Cambridge: CUP.

Searle, J. R. (1983). *Intentionality*. Cambridge: CUP.

Searle, J. R. (2002). *Consciousness and Language*. Cambridge: CUP.

Sebeok, T. A. (Ed.). (1960). *Style in Language*. Cambridge, MA: The MIT Press.

Shibamoto, J. (1980). Language Use and Linguistic Theory: Sexrelated variation in Japanese syntax. PhD thesis, University of California, Davis.

Shopen, T. (Ed.). (1985). *Language Typology and Syntactic Description*, 3 Vols. Cambridge: CUP.

Shore, S. (1988). On the so-called Finnish passive. *Word, 39* (3), 151–176.

Siewierska, A. (1991). *Functional Grammar*. London: Routledge.

Siewierska, A. (1993). Semantic functions and theta-roles: Convergences and divergences. *Working Papers in Functional Grammar, 55*, 1–21.

Silverstein, M. (1976). Hierarchy of features and ergativity. In Dixon (Ed.) 1976.

Slobin, D. (1996). From 'thought and language' to 'thinking for speaking'. In Gumperz & Levinson (Eds.) 1996.

Slobin, D. (2001). Form-function relations: How do children find out what they are? In Bowerman & Levinson (Eds.) 2001.

Sulkala, H. & M. Karjalainen (1992). *Finnish*. London: Routledge.

Suzuki, T. (1978). *Japanese and the Japanese* (translated by A. Miura). Tokyo: Kōdansha International.

Tagiuri, R. & L. Petrullo (Eds.). (1958). *Person Perception and Interpersonal Behavior*. Stanford, CA: Stanford University Press.

Talmy, L. (1983). How language structures space. In Pick & Acredolo (Eds.) 1983.

Talmy, L. (2000). *Toward a Cognitive Semantics*. Cambridge, MA: The MIT Press.

Tarantino, Q. (1994). *Pulp Fiction*. London: Faber & Faber.

Thalberg, I. (1972). *Enigmas of Agency*. London: George Allen & Unwin.

Thomas, J. (1995). *Meaning in Interaction: An introduction to pragmatics*. London: Longman.

Torn, R. (2002). The status of the passive in English and Estonian. *Working Papers in English and Applied Linguistics, 7*, 81–106. Cambridge: Research Centre for English and Applied Linguistics.

Triandis, H. C. (1988). Collectivism *vs.* individualism: A reconceptualization of a basic concept in cross-cultural psychology. In Verma & Bagley (Eds.) 1988.

Triandis, H. C. (1990). Cross-cultural studies of individualism-collectivism. In Berman (Ed.) 1990.

Tsujimura, N. (1996). *An Introduction to Japanese Linguistics*. Oxford: Basil Blackwell.

Tunmer, W. E. (1985). The acquisition of the sentient-nonsentient distinction and its relationship to causal reasoning and social cognition. *Child Development, 56*, 989–1000.

Van Oosten, J. (1984). Subject, topic, agent, and passive. PhD thesis, University of California, Berkeley.

Van Valin, R. D., Jr. (1985). Case marking and the structure of the Lhakhota clause. In Nichols & Woodbury (Eds.) 1985.

Verma, G. & C. Bagley (Eds.). (1988). *Cross-cultural studies of personality, attitudes and cognition*. London: MacMillan.

Weissenborn, J. & W. Klein (Eds.). (1982). *Here and There*. Amsterdam: John Benjamins.

Whorf, B. L. (1956). *Language, Thought, and Reality* (edited by J. B. Carroll). Cambridge, MA: The MIT Press.

Yamamoto, M. (1992a). The Manifestations of Person Deixis and Anaphora in English and Japanese. M.Phil. thesis, University of Cambridge.

Yamamoto, M. (1992b). Endophora and exophora in English and Japanese. *Doshisha Literature, 35*, 117–136.

Yamamoto, M. (1999). *Animacy and Reference: A cognitive approach to corpus linguistics*. Amsterdam: John Benjamins.

Yamamoto, M. (2000). Legitimacy of standard and nonstandard language in English and Japanese sociolinguistics: Focussing on socio-cultural relativity. *Doshisha Studies in Language and Culture, 2–4*, 659–687.

Yamamoto, M. (2003). *Igirisu no Michi: Fotojenikku-na Eikoku kigō-ron* (A Semiotics of Photogenic Britain: Her streets, footpaths and waterways). Tokyo: Shōhaku-sha.

Index

Studies in Language Companion Series

A complete list of titles in this series can be found on the publishers' website, *www.benjamins.com*

52 **TORRES CACOULLOS, Rena:** Grammaticization, Synchronic Variation, and Language Contact. A study of Spanish progressive -ndo constructions. 2000. xvi, 255 pp.

51 **ZIEGELER, Debra:** Hypothetical Modality. Grammaticalisation in an L2 dialect. 2000. xx, 290 pp.

50 **ABRAHAM, Werner and Leonid KULIKOV (eds.):** Tense-Aspect, Transitivity and Causativity. Essays in honour of Vladimir Nedjalkov. 1999. xxxiv, 359 pp.

49 **BHAT, D.N.S.:** The Prominence of Tense, Aspect and Mood. 1999. xii, 198 pp.

48 **MANNEY, Linda Joyce:** Middle Voice in Modern Greek. Meaning and function of an inflectional category. 2000. xiii, 262 pp.

47 **BRINTON, Laurel J. and Minoji AKIMOTO (eds.):** Collocational and Idiomatic Aspects of Composite Predicates in the History of English. 1999. xiv, 283 pp.

46 **YAMAMOTO, Mutsumi:** Animacy and Reference. A cognitive approach to corpus linguistics. 1999. xviii, 278 pp.

45 **COLLINS, Peter C. and David LEE (eds.):** The Clause in English. In honour of Rodney Huddleston. 1999. xv, 342 pp.

44 **HANNAY, Mike and A. Machtelt BOLKESTEIN (eds.):** Functional Grammar and Verbal Interaction. 1998. xii, 304 pp.

43 **OLBERTZ, Hella, Kees HENGEVELD and Jesús SÁNCHEZ GARCÍA (eds.):** The Structure of the Lexicon in Functional Grammar. 1998. xii, 312 pp.

42 **DARNELL, Michael, Edith MORAVCSIK, Michael NOONAN, Frederick J. NEWMEYER and Kathleen M. WHEATLEY (eds.):** Functionalism and Formalism in Linguistics. Volume II: Case studies. 1999. vi, 407 pp.

41 **DARNELL, Michael, Edith MORAVCSIK, Michael NOONAN, Frederick J. NEWMEYER and Kathleen M. WHEATLEY (eds.):** Functionalism and Formalism in Linguistics. Volume I: General papers. 1999. vi, 486 pp.

40 **BIRNER, Betty J. and Gregory WARD:** Information Status and Noncanonical Word Order in English. 1998. xiv, 314 pp.

39 **WANNER, Leo (ed.):** Recent Trends in Meaning–Text Theory. 1997. xx, 202 pp.

38 **HACKING, Jane F.:** Coding the Hypothetical. A comparative typology of Russian and Macedonian conditionals. 1998. vi, 156 pp.

37 **HARVEY, Mark and Nicholas REID (eds.):** Nominal Classification in Aboriginal Australia. 1997. x, 296 pp.

36 **KAMIO, Akio (ed.):** Directions in Functional Linguistics. 1997. xiii, 259 pp.

35 **MATSUMOTO, Yoshiko:** Noun-Modifying Constructions in Japanese. A frame semantic approach. 1997. viii, 204 pp.

34 **HATAV, Galia:** The Semantics of Aspect and Modality. Evidence from English and Biblical Hebrew. 1997. x, 224 pp.

33 **VELÁZQUEZ-CASTILLO, Maura:** The Grammar of Possession. Inalienability, incorporation and possessor ascension in Guaraní. 1996. xvi, 274 pp.

32 **FRAJZYNGIER, Zygmunt:** Grammaticalization of the Complex Sentence. A case study in Chadic. 1996. xviii, 501 pp.

31 **WANNER, Leo (ed.):** Lexical Functions in Lexicography and Natural Language Processing. 1996. xx, 355 pp.

30 **HUFFMAN, Alan:** The Categories of Grammar. French lui and le. 1997. xiv, 379 pp.

29 **ENGBERG-PEDERSEN, Elisabeth, Michael FORTESCUE, Peter HARDER, Lars HELTOFT and Lisbeth Falster JAKOBSEN (eds.):** Content, Expression and Structure. Studies in Danish functional grammar. 1996. xvi, 510 pp.

28 **HERMAN, József (ed.):** Linguistic Studies on Latin. Selected papers from the 6th International Colloquium on Latin Linguistics (Budapest, 23–27 March 1991). 1994. ix, 421 pp.

27 **ABRAHAM, Werner, T. GIVÓN and Sandra A. THOMPSON (eds.):** Discourse, Grammar and Typology. Papers in honor of John W.M. Verhaar. 1995. xx, 352 pp.

26 **LIMA, Susan D., Roberta L. CORRIGAN and Gregory K. IVERSON:** The Reality of Linguistic Rules. 1994. xxiii, 480 pp.

25 **GODDARD, Cliff and Anna WIERZBICKA (eds.):** Semantic and Lexical Universals. Theory and empirical findings. 1994. viii, 510 pp.

24 **BHAT, D.N.S.:** The Adjectival Category. Criteria for differentiation and identification. 1994. xii, 295 pp.

23 **COMRIE, Bernard and Maria POLINSKY (eds.):** Causatives and Transitivity. 1993. x, 399 pp.

22 **McGREGOR, William B.:** A Functional Grammar of Gooniyandi. 1990. xx, 618 pp.

21 **COLEMAN, Robert (ed.):** New Studies in Latin Linguistics. Proceedings of the 4th International Colloquium on Latin Linguistics, Cambridge, April 1987. 1990. x, 480 pp.